PIMLICO

44

JOHN MASEFIELD

Muriel Spark is celebrated as a novelist and as a playwright, a biographer, a writer of children's books and a poet. Her novel, *The Prime of Miss Jean Brodie* (1961) was adapted for stage, cinema and TV. Several of her books have been made into films, the last one being *The Abbess of Crewe* in 1974. She was awarded the James Tait Black Memorial Prize for her novel *The Mandelbaum Gate* (1956). Her most recent novel, *Symposium*, was published in 1990.

Muriel Spark was educated in Edinburgh, lived in London after the war and now lives in Italy.

JOHN MASEFIELD

MURIEL SPARK

PIMLICO

PIMLICO

20 Vauxhall Bridge Road, London SW1V 2SA

London Melbourne Sydney Auckland Johannesburg
and agencies throughout the world

First published 1953
Revised edition 1962
This new edition first published by Hutchinson 1991
Pimlico edition 1992

Photoset by Raven Typesetters, Ellesmere Port, South Wirral

Printed and bound in Great Britain by
Mackays of Chatham PLC, Chatham, Kent

ISBN 0–7126–5247–7

Contents

Introduction (1991)

In the 1960s I went to see Wystan Auden, and found him rewriting some of his poetry of the late 1930s. I suggested that he was overlaying his thoughts of that time with his thoughts of thirty years later. He replied that in fact he wasn't doing any such thing. He was expressing what he had thought and felt more precisely now than he had been able to do at the time.

I thought of Auden's words when I came to revise books like the present one on John Masefield which was a work of my maturing mind; I believe it has something of my own to offer the reader and the student of the subject. I wrote *John Masefield* in the years 1951–1952. The work was published in 1953 and reissued in 1962, and I have confined myself to making more clear what I meant at the time. I was happy when the first reviewers of the book discerned that, labour of love though it was, it was honest and never fulsome.

Since this book was first published two important books on Masefield have appeared: *John Masefield, A Life* (1978) by Constance Babington Smith, which is an excellent and full-scale biography, and *John Masefield's England* (1973) by Professor Fraser Drew, a splendid portrait of Masefield as a chronicler of England. I hope the present work, concentrating as it does on Masefield's narrative powers, will contribute to the picture of a remarkable man and writer.

Towards the end of 1950 I was still a fairly unknown writer, a poet and critic. My poetry was moving more and more towards the narrative form. I was not yet ready to write novels. I thought in many ways that novels were a lazy way of writing poetry, and above all I didn't want to become a 'lady-novelist' with all the slop and sentimentalism that went with that classification. (In that aim, at least, I have the satisfaction of having been successful.)

Although I now write novels, and only occasional poems, I still think of myself as a narrative poet. My novels are not verse, they are not poetic in the flowery sense. But I claim a poetic perception, a poet's way of looking at the world, a synoptic vision.

Looking back at this work I wrote on Masefield, I feel a large amount of my writing on him can be applied generally; it is in many ways a statement of my position as a literary critic and I hope some readers will recognize it as such. Certainly I have changed over the intervening years, but my basic tenets remain surprisingly (even to me) constant.

I wrote to Masefield on 28th November, 1950, suggesting the book. He was the Poet Laureate, still in the public mind the 'sailor-poet', but at that time not very widely read. I felt he was overlooked for the wrong reasons. Masefield replied immediately in his characteristically courteous manner:

> I am much honoured, that you should wish to write about my work, and much touched that you should have read so much of it and continue its friend.
>
> Would it be too much to ask, that you should first meet and talk with me?

I arranged to visit John Masefield at his house, Burcote Brook, Abingdon in Berkshire on 6 December 1950. He sent a car to meet me at Oxford Station. It was a freezing day. The snow was deep. Here is the account of my meeting with Masefield that I wrote in my Memorandum Book:

> *Dec. 8 1950*
> In bed with cold which was caught at Abingdon, and I can't help thinking that if Masefield were not so intemperately

'Temperant' I would not be snuffling and choking thus – i.e. if he had offered me a drink on frozen Wednesday last. But I have not the heart to blame him for in all else he is a generous and delightful host.

He has a large house, much larger than I expected, with a lodge and drive. Somehow, I didn't expect to find the atmosphere of comfort and success. A lovely-looking old man. Rosy cheeks, white skin, pure-white hair and moustache and blue, blue eyes. A charming voice which carefully enunciates all vowels and speaks boldly. First I was shown into his study which looks out on a long stretch of grass (frosted over on Wednesday) leading to a river running between clumps of trees. There was a large fire, comfortable chairs into one of which I was put, but M. chose a hard armless chair which he seemed to prefer (like the Admiral in 'Dead Ned'). He asked me kindly about my journey; then spoke about Mary Shelley (on whom I had told him by letter I had written), and whom he described as an excellent widow, whatever kind of wife she made. He spoke of Shelley and his admiration for his work, though he (M.) 'did not think all priests and kings were evil'. Then of Godwin whom he disliked, he said, although he had read and enjoyed his novels when young. I asked if *Caleb Williams* had influenced 'Dead Ned' and he replied, yes possibly, though he was not aware of it & in fact could not remember the story. The idea of 'Dead Ned'; he told me, was given him by a story he was told when dining at Barber Surgeons' Hall. He was informed that the very table on which he was dining was that used formerly by the dissectors of hanged men, who had been condemned to be drawn and quartered, and exposed to public view. The surgeons who performed this office were under the secret oath of their society, to try to restore life whenever one of the hanged bodies showed signs of life (as frequently happened). M. was shown an oriental screen which had been sent by one of the criminals who had there been revived, to his surgeon-benefactors. It was the custom that when this reviving of the hanged took place, they were shipped abroad, just like Dead Ned. M. said that his brother had found some papers relating to some criminal who survived hanging and escaped rehanging through a pardon. These stories went to the making of the novel.

He asked me a little about myself, but did not seem too

curious. I told him a few brief details. He said how touched he was by my wishing to write the book, and I told him part of my plan. He said, in reference to *Dauber* that the story was told him exactly as it is recounted in the poem, even to the dying words of the Dauber 'It will go on.' He said he did not think much of *Dauber* either way, it was written so long ago. *The Everlasting Mercy*, he said, was of course a turning point in his career. (He did not seem keen to talk about his work, and so much that I wanted to ask him will now have to be put to him by letter.)

He spoke then of Rossetti and asked, I think, what is thought of him now. I said there is a tendency to think of him as a languishing aesthete. He said 'Oh but when I was a young poet we looked upon Rossetti as the life force of poetry. Without Rossetti, Swinburne could not have been, William Morris could not have been, Burne Jones could not have been.' He went out to fetch Mrs Masefield whom I shall describe presently, then continued, 'Without Rossetti they would all have been clergy-men – Swinburne would have been a curate.' Mrs M. laughed – a high cackle as is the laugh of the deaf, sometimes – and said, 'Imagine Swinburne a curate.' Masefield then spoke of Rossetti's discovery of Fitzgerald and the enormous success of *Rubaiyat*. Every copy was sold and they were selling at a pound a-piece (originally the book was a farthing) until the day the copyright was released when about six publishers brought out Omar and once again they went into edition after edition. Mrs Masefield left the study to go and finish her letter and about ten minutes before lunch we joined her in a smaller room which had a smaller fire, burning logs and peat. She, too, preferred a low hard chair as she said she always wanted to fall asleep in a soft chair. She was a small, kindly person, very weird-looking, with an ear-apparatus and glasses that looked as if they covered one glass eye – at least one eye had a special lens that magnified the eye to look like a marble. She was dressed in an antique black hat trimmed with velvet, a red jersey and shortish old-fashioned grey skirt. Her voice was rather appalling, being due no doubt to some deafness. I liked her; and Masefield behaved with natural courtesy towards her. I should think she has been a true companion to him. They talked of their travels, from time to time, speaking of the lion farm at Hollywood, which Masefield said was kept specially for film use. He had seen one shot of a film introducing lions and Christians in the Roman arena. The lions were trained not to eat people, only to look fierce, but, he said, the Christians in this particular film would have put any healthy lion off.

We went into lunch – had some fricassee, very well cooked, accompanied by vegetables and 'delights' as Masefield called them. These 'delights' were pecan nuts and raisins. During lunch Masefield told me how he had hung round Swinburne's door at Putney as a young man to see the poet – a queer figure with an auriole of red hair, tripping up Putney Hill. He asked, what did I think of Swinburne! I said I appreciated his technique but could not really extend my enjoyment beyond the words. He said, to the young poets at the end of the last century, Swinburne seemed to have released the language – he could do anything with language.

Meanwhile, I was feeling rather cold. We were all three provided with a black shiny round oil stove, reaching about 2 ft. But the other side was cold. Anyway, we returned to the smaller drawing-room after eating Christmas pudding which M. said he hoped was my first time this year. There in the smaller room, we had coffee which M. poured and served; and he was very assiduous in pressing me to further 'delights' – fruit sweets, etc.

Other things he had told me during this time were: that he couldn't get beyond a few pages of *Wuthering Heights*, although he admired what Rossetti had said of it – 'The characters speak English but the scene is apparently laid in Hell.' *Jane Eyre*, he said, was considered a wicked book in his youth and his sister was forbidden to read it. He believed, he said, that he read a lot of books in his youth which would have been forbidden him 'had they known'; he told me, too, that he thought the present poor sales of poetry were due to the high price of the books. He considered that the theory was wrong which attributed the unpopularity of poetry to inferior work by present-day poets, for, he said, the public for poetry has actually increased; Yeats, he said, estimated the British poetry-reading public at 4,000. – Today, there are 1 million B.B.C. listeners to poetry programmes.

I left him at 2 p.m. – his car was waiting to take me into Oxford. I left him with a feeling of unexpected warmth. He had given me two of his photographs and his 'Book of Both Sorts' inscribed to me; and had said that he would give me every help with my book. A new autobiographical book by him is appearing in April – first in the *Atlantic Monthly* as a serial – but apart from my use of the material in this book, in 'The Conway' and 'In the Mill', he promised to 'think up' new material for me.

Throughout, he was most unaffectedly gracious kind and sweet – an absolute poppet. I had rather expected to find a denunciatory reactionary somewhat out of sorts with the world & soured by neglect. Not a bit of it. His interest in all varieties of life's manifestations is still avid – much more so than mine or most of my generation's will ever be. The inner life of the man has not swallowed up the outer life. He is a poet of outwardness – of the essence of reality, not the essence of illusion. A born story-teller (as Herbert Palmer writes) – and this is true of his conversation as well as his art.

The car dropped me at Broad Street. It was just before 2.30. I dived into a basement tavern next door to Blackwell's and knocked back a double rum. Even so, I have a cold from my day's excursion.

One of the things I found very charming about Masefield was his interest in my tartan dress, which led him to look up the colours in a book, *Clans & Tartans of Scotland*: it is that of the MacKenzies. The war-cry was given as 'Tulach Ard', which fascinated Masefield. He repeated it over and over.

Dec. 9. Masefield also remarked on the true greatness of *Jude the Obscure*. I have remembered, too, that Masefield said that the theme of *Dauber* was that the artist is compelled to obey the law of his own being, no matter if death or disaster ensues.

Dec. 9. (evening). I have just remembered more things about my visit to Masefield.

1) He began by asking me if I had a good journey, and had I much trouble getting from my home to Paddington.

2) He admires Peacock's poems, especially mentioning 'The Three Wise Men' and 'War Song'.

3) Re. 'Dead Ned' – he said he had a special interest in the Coast of Dead Ned, about which it is said,

> Beware, beware, the Bight of Benin,
> Few come out, though many go in.

4) He said that recently he had been reading some of Tom

Moore's poems, and found some of them surprisingly good, though, he said 'We used to mock them.'

5) He spoke about the suitability of the apron-stage to Elizabethan drama. He wondered why the Roman theatre at Verulamium had not been used for theatre purposes – for some open-air drama. Why not a circus – 'Bertram Mills at the Roman Theatre,' he said half-humorously.

6) When I told him I sometimes take a part-time job he said, 'All experience is good for an artist.' I felt flattered – about the 'artist' bit.

I wrote to thank the Masefields for their kindness. Masefield replied with the letter from which I have quoted on p. 41, reiterating the effect of Rossetti and Swinburne on a young poet like himself. He ended the letter hoping that the cry of 'Tulach Ard!' would continue to echo up the Old Brompton Road.

Masefield was born in 1878. He was 72 when I met him, at that time recovering from a serious illness. But he always found time to reply to my queries and to make helpful suggestions. When my book was finally completed I know he was pleased with it:

> Please let me thank you for the patient care with which you have worked at my things, & for the generous things you have written.
>   Please forgive me, will you, if I add, after these thanks, (so well deserved by you), that I find a book about myself most difficult to read. 'What a pity,' I keep saying, 'that this Lady had not a better subject.'

I did not meet John Masefield again till the mid-sixties. He was now well over eighty and rather frail. He had attended a poetry reading and was sitting with some friends. I approached to greet him, begging him not to get up. But he stood up straight in his usual manner. He was brimming with pleasure about my successes, for by that time my early novels had been published. 'Your name is all over the place!' he said. We spoke for a while about those days, fifteen years before, when I wrote the present essay, *John Masefield.*

Introduction (1952)

John Masefield is known to all of us, known as the Poet Laureate, known as the author of a great many poems, plays, novels and historical works – but known mainly as the laureate and associated with his poems. I do not think there is any need of a book to make him wider known.

As to my reasons, then, for writing this book. First, I was strongly attracted by John Masefield's narrative art, and I wished this exclusive aspect of the poet to be more closely considered. And then, I had the impression that, because the poet had been writing so much, for so long, and about so many things, and perhaps because he is a poet laureate, and because he is very often, erroneously, thought of as a 'Georgian' poet,[1] he does not receive sufficient attention in the capacity in which he excels, that is, as a story-teller.

A word about the plan of the book. Masefield has written abundantly in a variety of forms and on a multitude of subjects. I confine myself to those writings which, for reasons elaborated in later chapters, I feel are relevant to his development as a story-teller, or which I think are durable.

My first task, in a general chapter on John Masefield's work, is to dissociate him from the category of the Georgian Group, for, to many people, the belief that he is 'one of the Georgians' is an obstacle between them and his work. The time is perhaps already past when it was a kind of calumny to regard a poet as a Georgian; an attitude of hostility towards Georgian verse has been replaced by one of apathy on the

[1]The term 'Georgian' is used always with reference to the Georgian Anthology group, and other contemporaries of its kind.

part of critics, which I dare say is just; the only point I wish to make is, that it is inaccurate to include John Masefield's work in the genre for which the Georgian poets were famed. In making a general assessment of his work, in the first chapter, I attempt also to focus attention on aspects which earlier generations overlooked or disliked, and which a later sensibility may recognize and admire.

The other chapters are devoted to the development of the poet's achievements in narrative writing. In the biographical chapter I try to bring out some of that abundant capacity for *experiencing* which Masefield's novels and narrative poems show. Those parts of his life story which the poet himself has written about never fail to give the impression that life has always presented itself to him in the narrative form. About story-telling the poet has written: '. . . As it has been the law of my being, I have followed it, and have given to it whatever effort I could give . . . I have always been able to take risks in order to do the work of story-telling.'[1]

I ought to explain why I deal more fully with the two early books of short poems than with those sonnets and lyrics which appeared after the publication of *The Everlasting Mercy* in 1911. These early verses – *Salt Water Ballads* especially – seem to reveal the narrative poet in the making; they show the novelist in the making as well. I might perhaps have been expected to give more attention to the sonnets than I do. The sonnets represent, to many readers, the poet's best work. But after some hesitation I decided to treat them here in the way in which I have always regarded them – as personal statements. The sonnets are the poet's attempt to clarify his thought and to formulate a philosophy. In my view, the poet's 'philosophy' is more vividly disclosed through the narrative verse, and I do not think the sonnet sequence, for all its competence, is in direct relationship with John Masefield's narrative genius. But as personal statements these sonnets are of considerable importance, and as such are examined in the biographical chapter. As to the later

[1]*So Long to Learn* (Heinemann 1952).

lyrics, again, I do not conceive them to be in the main line of my subject, namely, John Masefield as story-teller. Besides, I cannot regard the verbal quality of these sonnets and lyrics without some degree of fidgeting animadversion. The extreme unevenness of Masefield's poetry is a point which all his critics must consider.

It is with the narrative poems that I feel not only at ease but deeply engaged. After a general statement on narrative poetry, I thought it right to examine closely and at length what I believe to be Masefield's three main works, *The Everlasting Mercy*, *Dauber* and *Reynard the Fox*; and I end with a chapter on his narrative prose.

Though his dramatic works have undoubtedly played a large part in the poet's growth as a teller of stories, I do not take them into account here, and this advisedly, since, as the poet himself insists, he has no talent for play writing. I do not think the plays have lasting value or will enjoy a revival, in the sense that the three narrative poems I have just mentioned are assured of a permanent place in the history of English Literature. And it would be outside the scope of this book to bring the type of criticism to bear on these plays which drama demands. For like reason many excellent and valuable books, as I am told, but of which I am not myself competent to judge, are not discussed here – such books as *Agriculture in the Colonies* and *My Faith in Women's Suffrage* among many others. And for this reason I have not dealt fully with the war histories, though it should be observed that Masefield's prose is always, whatever purpose it is adapted to, a joy to read. And, when he is writing, as in the war histories, of national events on the grand scale, there are times when he seems inspired to interpret the function of laureate in a higher manner than that revealed by his state-occasion verses which appear now and then in the newspapers.

In fact, what I am concerned with in this book represents only a fraction of John Masefield's work; and my excuse is, that I am looking for two things: the best work and the narrative art. Almost invariably the two things coincide.

One

Masefield's Achievement

I

To agree with the claim[1] that John Masefield was the first of the 'Georgians' would seem to me more difficult than to disagree with those who in 1911 declared that *The Everlasting Mercy* was not poetry. I mean that, if *The Everlasting Mercy* is not poetry, then it is something else of a vital and original order. For the term 'poetry' is one whose meaning can become debased by too exalted an application, and if we allow it to bask in that comfortable paradox, we are forced to admit that there are some poems in which 'poetry' has no place. But the truth is, that in 1911 the minority who would not call this poem a poem, found in it a quality they were not accustomed to finding in poetry at all, the special quality of realism which we now take for granted as one of the resources of verse.

But to say that Masefield is the first of the Georgians is to make a statement worth challenging and worth examining, because I believe it to reveal a fallacy in the general idea of what his poetry really is. 'He is certainly no true-blue Georgian,' wrote Herbert Palmer.[2] But I hope to show that he is no Georgian at all.

Masefield could in any case only be called a Georgian in retrospect. He began writing, and was known, before the

[1] cf *The Georgian Literary Scene* by Frank Swinnerton (1935).
[2] *Post-Victorian Poetry* by Herbert Palmer (1938).

1

Georgian poets assembled themselves into a group. Most of them regarded him with suspicion if not with hostility. That he was represented (comparatively seldom) in the early numbers of Sir Edward Marsh's Georgian anthologies means very little, if we remember that D.H. Lawrence had also a place there. John Masefield is as little a Georgian poet as is Lawrence. So it was a quality in his work noticed some twenty years after the Georgian movement began, but not noticed at the time, which caused the critic to suggest that *The Everlasting Mercy* started 'all the excitement' and hence the Georgian movement. Excitement the poem certainly caused, among so miscellaneous a public that the Georgian poets may have benefited from the widened public interest in poetry which John Masefield's poem created. But that is a superficial connection between *The Everlasting Mercy* and Georgian Anthology work. Sir Edward Marsh's flock were domestic-rural. They were highly expressive about hedges and ditches, cups of tea and pints of stout; they were taken up with humane feelings and they were irresponsible. *The Everlasting Mercy* is not the same thing in a larger manifestation; the poem is composed of dramatic, demonstrable elements which amount to a life-size meaning.

The general way of looking at John Masefield's poetry differs from the way it was thought of before the Georgian taste[1] set in. That is, many critics saw only those aspects of his work conformable or otherwise to Georgian standards. But there are sides of Masefield's work which nothing the Georgians wrote, or that has been written before and after, can approximate to. It has the vitality to be remarked in such poets as Swinburne and Kipling; but with a range of human experience lacking in Swinburne, a broad-minded sense of proportion lacking in Kipling; and naturalness of expression lacking in so vigorous a poet as Browning.

This vitality was overwhelmingly felt when *The Everlasting*

[1] *'Georgian taste': the kind of taste formulated, belatedly, in 1933 by A. E. Housman's Name and Nature of Poetry.*

Mercy appeared in 1911. The vitality was felt but its source never quite located, which I think caused some confusion in the ensuing controversy as to the merits and demerits of the work. Many people have recorded the reception of this poem. For a work of art, it was discussed with a heat almost unnatural in an English public; the following passage describes the impact of *The Everlasting Mercy*:

> In 1911 Masefield was a comparatively unknown writer, and when in that year he sent a poem (*The Everlasting Mercy*) of enormous dimensions to the *English Review* there was consternation in the offices. The editors, Austin Harrison and Norman Douglas, liked it mightily, but it was too long, a third the length of any issue of the *English Review*. Moreover it was full of oaths and curses, language to shock every drawing-room and literary *salon*. They were terrified of it. But how stirring it seemed! What was to be done? Should they attempt it? They did; and the *English Review* went straightway out of print. Masefield was made for life, and the *English Review* increased its circulation. Then the publishers Sidgwick & Jackson reprinted the poem in book form, and it went into edition after edition. The reviewers cursed and blessed it, and the Nonconformist clergy quoted from it in their Sunday sermons. It was even a bigger literary sensation than Kipling's *Barrack Room Ballads*[1].

I don't mean to base any of my claims for John Masefield on the situation described above. There has never been anything about a literary or social sensation that proves the durability of anything. But what it does prove is that an unusual number of the poetry-reading public, as well as the public which does not normally read poetry became conscious of Masefield in 1911; and attached to his reputation was an idea, unwittingly fostered by the enthusiasts as well as the denouncers, of his type of writing. It was not altogether the wrong idea, but it was not a critical one.

The predominant conception of John Masefield formed at

[1] *Post-Victorian Poetry* (Herbert Palmer).

this time was, that with *The Everlasting Mercy* he had done something in poetry which liberated the feelings of the reader. He had brought about a wholesale catharsis. And this is a fact, as we have seen. Where the confusion arose, and where the error occurred in what I have called the Masefield 'idea' was over the more properly critical question of how he achieved this effect. Readers of English poetry at the time were not used to having their feelings exalted or, as some felt, outraged, by a poem so entirely impersonal as *The Everlasting Mercy*. In all the discussion there seems to have been very little assessment of what the poem really is: an objective account of sin and salvation as it existed in the life of an English rustic youth of the mid-nineteenth century. No one was prepared for such objective realism. It was assumed that the poem came straight from the heart of the author, which it did of course; but with this assumption went the further one that it was an exhilarating piece of propaganda for the evangelical cause which, as I see it, the poem is not. Intellectually, most people grasped that the poem represented 'realism', but emotionally the readers were not attuned to realism, especially in so passionate a poem. It was a new type of writing, and that always takes a long time to be properly understood.

That is why the sophisticates raised their eyebrows and the Nonconformist clergy hurled stanzas of the poem from their pulpits. One significant symptom of this one-sided view was the childish concern which critics, favourable and adverse, had with the pub scenes, or with the hells and bloodies in the poem. On the one hand, the feeling was that here at last was *real* realism, since realism, it was supposed, must be something sordid; or again, it was argued that the poem was downright disgraceful. The most soberly appreciative reviews were frequently followed by indignant letters centring round this question of the bloodies. Lord Alfred Douglas, presumably acting on the principle that attack is the best form of defence, was long and loud in his complaints

– the poem was 'nine-tenths sheer filth'; Masefield exceeded even Marlowe's 'wicked licentiousness', and so on. Not the whole of the controversy was conducted on these lines, but an amazing amount of it was.

Perhaps the most revealing report of the argument was this:

> It started excitement because upon its publication nobody could positively decide for all whether it was good or not. It was vehement, the language used by some of the persons depicted in it had all the air of being obscene (e.g. 'you closhy put' which proved to be disappointingly mild), the revivalist fervour of the later pages was to some very moving, and in fact those who prided themselves on their fastidiousness were compelled to read it in order the better to ridicule it.[1]

It was not the poem that was in question at all – not the aptness of the language to the narrative, but whether or not it was obscene; not the appropriateness of the revivalist fervour to the character who experienced it, but whether or not revivalist fervour was acceptable. While these critics were exclaiming over the naughtiness of it all, while they were expressing the refinements of their own feelings, the real audacity of the poem, the all-over realism of it, was overlooked. The real audacity has nothing to do with oaths and curses and pub scenes, but in the rhythm, the arrangement, the verbal development, of lines like

> 'It's mine.'
> 'It ain't.'
> 'You put.'
> 'You liar.'
> 'You closhy put.'
> 'You bloody liar.'

which was something altogether unpredicted. It is ordinary

[1] *The Georgian Literary Scene* (Swinnerton).

speech in so far as it depicts the way in which two country youths of the time and locality might be expected to argue; but there is artistic realism in the conversation which is quite apart from historical accuracy; it is ordinary speech and also poetic speech, how attained? The poetic effect depends here on the dramatic effect, and even within the limits of this small quotation the technique of dramatic art can be detected. The effect clearly does not derive from dialectic strength, nor does it come from the comparatively mild vituperative language. It is a matter of rhythmic balance, where the stresses shift from line to line. Consider the passage set out like this:

> It's mine / It ain't / You put / You liar
> You closhy put / You bloody liar.

In proportion as the staccato sentences in the first line are elongated in the second, so do mood and meaning develop beyond the mere qualifying value of the adjective: an aural suggestiveness induced by changing accentuation and by repetition overlies the verbal meaning.

I give this isolated example because I think that the shock felt by Masefield's readers forty years ago was partly due to the newness and unexpectedness of his technique. Not that the lines quoted above are in any sense typical of his work; they do not represent one of his tricks – but he is to be recognized at his best, when he so arranges common speech that it becomes poetic speech, and without that display of effort which marks stylized poetry. By now we are used to hearing ordinary language made poetic by rhythmic arrangement:

Doris: I like Sam.
Dusty: *I* like Sam
             Yes and Sam's a nice boy too.
             He's a funny fellow.

6

Doris:	He *is* a funny fellow.

. . . . . .

Dusty:	The Knave of Spades.
Doris:	That'll be Snow.
Dusty:	Or it might be Swarts.
Doris:	Or it might be Snow.[1]

There was also, as one critic said, a doubt whether *The Everlasting Mercy* 'was good or not'. The originality of the poem caused the doubt, and that originality was not only a question of technique. It was not clear to readers long accustomed to subjective verse, whether the poet identified himself with his character Saul Kane; whether, in fact, he had himself experienced Saul Kane's conversation. Mostly they thought he had; some heartily approved, others thought it would never do. This attitude was borne out after *Reynard the Fox* appeared to attract even wider popularity. Whose side was the poet on, many people wondered, that of the hunters or the fox? That question should not have arisen at all in connection with the poem, but it did arise. Herbert Palmer wrote, 'In *Reynard the Fox*, a poem of many facets, the hunted and harassed human being is symbolized – as a fox. And the fox gets off.'[2] That is hardly so. The poem is not of the many-faceted order of poetry; it is depicted with intensity on a single level of experience. The fox is no symbol, but a very fox. In *Reynard* the poet's sympathy is with the fox equally with the many and miscellaneous human characters; the story is the thing. With the exception of *Dauber*, Masefield's narrative verse does not lend itself to a symbolist approach. It is not the sort of poetry which can be interpreted in several ways; it is the poetry of the surface; and this is not to imply a distinction in merit, but in kind. For Masefield's view of the surface of life is comprehensive.

[1] *Sweeney Agonistes* by T.S. Eliot (*Collected Poems* 1942 edn.).
[2] *Post-Victorian Poetry.*

There is no limit or stipulation attached to the impressions he is prepared to receive. His subject-matter is everything on the face of the earth. We are not therefore to look in his work for a vision of Heaven-on-Earth, as we look in Blake; or for a vision of Hell-on-Earth, as we do in Baudelaire (to mention extreme examples). We must look for a vision of terrestrial life: a vision of its uniqueness and its unity.

It should be said that a great many critics paid lip-service to his 'objectivity'. But the degree of his objectivity was not thoroughly comprehended; even the wittiest parodists of *The Everlasting Mercy* assumed that the poet was secretly a benign patron to Saul Kane; the parodies failed, for they did not stab to the heart.

I would not like to be understood to be making out a general case for objectivity in poetry; only for a full understanding of the extent to which it is present in Masefield's writings. Browning defined the objective poet as 'one whose endeavour has been to produce things external (whether the phenomena of the scenic universe, or the manifested action of the human heart and brain) with an immediate reference, in every case, to the common eye and apprehension of his fellow-men, assumed capable of receiving and profiting by this reproduction'.[1] There is in this definition that which Browning himself can be seen to have aimed at, though often failing to keep Browning out of the picture. The words can be applied accurately, though not as an inclusive statement, to John Masefield; and where Browning comes nearest to the definition he anticipates an aspect of Masefield. One of the first to recognize an affinity between these poets was an early critic who made the point, as I have done, in order to draw a distinction between Browning and Masefield.

Everyone has read Browning's lines about 'the wild joys of

[1]Browning's *Introduction* (1852, later withdrawn) to the Shelley letters which proved to be forgeries.

living, the leaping from rock up to rock'. These are splendid lines: but one somehow does not feel that Browning ever leapt from rock up to rock himself. He saw other people doing it, doubtless, and thought it fine. But I don't think he did it himself ever. . . .

Masefield writes that he knows and testifies that he has seen. Throughout his poems there are lines and phrases so instinct with life that they betoken a man who writes of what he has experienced, not of what he thinks he can imagine. . . .[1]

This returns us to the consideration which occupied so many of John Masefield's critics: the place of personal experience in his poetry. It is partly true that: 'Masefield writes that he knows and testifies that he has seen.' Masefield has enjoyed a great number of uncommon experiences and they give conviction to his work. But between his actual experiences and those he has imaginatively apprehended, we can draw no line, for he is equally convincing when recounting either, or a mixture of both. This partial truth is to be found in something else the critic said of John Masefield – 'He is a man of action not imagination.' This is apparently nonsense – a 'man of action not imagination' could not win a battle far less write a poem. But Masefield is indeed a man of action, and he is a man of imagination as well. It might more correctly be said: Browning depicted human action in terms of poetic thought; Masefield depicts poetic thought in terms of human action. And if this is true, as I think it is, then the property which has immediate reference to the 'common eye and apprehension of his fellowmen', as Browning has it, is in Masefield's case, action; in Browning's, poetic thought. It needs no elaboration of this to show that action has more immediate reference than has poetic thought; that is why Browning's attempts at objectivity, particularly in narrative form, show an obvious strain. Masefield's manner of conveying external things is comparatively effortless, and this, I

[1]From the essay on John Masefield by C. H. Sorley, added to the third edition of his *Marlborough and other Poems* (1916).

think, causes the fallacy which prompted some of his contemporaries to think of him as a man of action who simply recorded things seen and done by him. Because he conveys human action with such immediate simplicity, it rather seems as if this is the case; indeed this impression signifies one of the essentials of his art; but it is not so. Whatever events of his life are reflected in his work are transformed by his imaginative grasp of them, they are changed by an intense vision of wholeness which does not attach to individual happenings in real life; and it is the vision, not the event, which is revealed to us finally in terms of action. That is the objectivity of Masefield, as I see it, and that is where he is unique.

I have dwelt at this length on the impressions he made on his contemporaries because I have felt that while there were elements of sound judgment in their responses, they were confused by a general approach to poetry which I do not think altogether the right one where Masefield's writings are concerned. I do not suggest that my own approach is the 'right' one either, nor that anything so changeable as literary sensibility can at any point in time be called absolutely right or wrong. I have merely thought it time now for a reassessment of a poet whose reputation was so rapidly and strongly established that he became a fashion. And it has hardly been questioned whether the Poet Laureate is truly represented by that past fashion, whether what he has created is of lasting value, and if so, in what portion of his work.

II

The truest thing that has been said of Masefield, and the most frequent, is that he is a 'born story-teller'. In an address on Chaucer, he once said:

Let me speak to you of Chaucer to-day not as a learned man nor as one interested in the fourteenth century; but as one fond of stories and interested in all ways of telling them and in all systems of arranging them when told.

People tell stories because they have a genius for it. People listen to stories, because life is so prone to action that the very shadow of action will sway the minds of men and women: any purpose will arrest no purpose.[1]

That he is a born story-teller is apparent, not only from the fact that he is at his best when telling a story, but from his confident way – whether in the form of verse, novel or historical record – of attacking a tale and spinning it out, his way of bringing a story immediately before his audience. He takes for granted a larger and more receptive audience than most men of letters have the courage or justification to do. He addresses, not only the inquiring, the bookish or the purposive minds, but those with no particular purpose, and does so with effect. This alone makes for uniqueness. As one who adapts a story-telling capacity to several art-forms, he is distinctive in our time, when the art of narrative is almost entirely confined to the novel, which at its best has become confined to the narrative of ideas. His own novels I look upon as aspects of a poet; and as a narrator in prose and verse he can best be compared with other narrative poets. In this sense, he is unique not only in our own time, but in the period extending back to Chaucer, for though during that time the novel form has evolved and developed, though poetic narrative is by no means scarce in our literature following Chaucer, there is nowhere – not in Spenser, in Crabbe, Burns, Byron, Browning or William Morris (to name but a few narrative poets) – such purity of motive and in such abundance, as in Chaucer and in Masefield. There are likewise refinements in the narrative verse of the six centuries which lie between these poets, which both lack;

[1] From an essay on Chaucer published in *Recent Prose* by John Masefield (revised ed., 1932).

11

and there are differences between Chaucer and Masefield which demand examination; but I am concerned here with Masefield's historical importance, so far as he possesses this purity of motive combined with abundance which had disappeared from English poetry for so long a time. 'He brought us to reading Chaucer over again,' Middleton Murry admitted in the course of differentiating between Chaucer and Masefield.[1]

The motive behind Masefield's narrative art is pure because it is apparently designed simply to convey a story in the most pleasurable and memorable form, without emphasis on moral, political or religious issues or issues personal to the poet. That is not to say that moral, political, religious or personal themes do not exist in his work; only that they are not emphasized by a didactic intention.

The abundance of Masefield's work is something that must be reckoned with, not in a spirit of quantitative judgment, but with the thought in mind that the abundance, in such variety as Masefield has given, is by itself a telling thing. In my own opinion he has produced a superfluity of writing; but there remains an abundance which is not superfluous and which betokens the uniqueness I speak of when allied to a sustained purity of narrative method. From well over a hundred publications which include poems, plays, historical episodes of the two world wars, verse and prose anthologies, essays, lectures, books on agriculture, on Shakespeare, on Rossetti, on ships and shipping, he emerges as a later type of epic writer; in which respect, of course, his resemblance to Chaucer ends.

In his documentary account of the evacuation of Dun-kirk,[2] Masefield writes, 'The people of this island . . . have cared a good deal for what will look well in a ballad.' And that too, is really the essence of John Masefield's writings; he

[1] *The Nostalgia of Mr. Masefield* in *Aspects of Literature*, J. Middleton Murry (1920).
[2] *The Nine Days' Wonder* (1941).

cares a good deal for what will look well in a ballad, no matter what form of writing he uses for the purpose. (He seldom, in fact, uses the ballad form.) He is an objective, comprehensive and liberal observer of humanity and all the activities of man. He is not concerned with putting forward those individual impressions of society which have indeed enriched European literature; he is occupied with a vision of things – not a vision in the idealized sense, but a vision of things as they are as distinct from things as they sound in factual reportage. He concentrates therefore on those aspects of man and nature which signify, which look well in a ballad. Not that his work is stamped with the heroic spirit, as we take the phrase from the vocabulary of the critics; but that the poet evokes an heroic spirit nearer the life-size than the heroic spirit proper; and he does this through his reverence for humanity's powers of endurance, imagination and skill.

Now this high sense of man's vocation is the sort of thing politicians and suchlike are always talking about and so we are not to be blamed if we regard with boredom, if not with suspicion, the talking about it by anyone else. There is also poetry in plenty to express these humanist sentiments, but it has been difficult for any poet since the eighteenth century to get away with it. Masefield does not always get away with it, but predominantly he does; and this is because he manages to steer between classical heroics and the spirit of the age as interpreted by, for example, J. B. Priestley.

Masefield re-introduced flesh-and-blood into poetry. It will be said, what of Kipling? Kipling, it is true, dealt in flesh-and-blood but, with all respect to the tendency inaugurated by T. S. Eliot, to do Kipling's verse justice, I do not mean the kind of flesh-and-blood Kipling dealt in. For Kipling had little respect for flesh-and-blood, and you might argue in his favour that his respect was for God, not man. But if you say this, you must remember that it was reverence tainted with pride, tempered only intermittently by an humble and a contrite heart: the humility was expressed after the bombast had been elaborated upon with evident relish. Kipling's God, moreover, is not a God of immanence, but is remote and judicious, somewhat like Kipling. The flesh-and-blood remains, with Kipling, as carnal as those bare words sound and therefore up to no particular good, as he, uniquely in his own way, saw it. But 'flesh-and-blood' is not as carnal as it sounds. And so when I say it was Masefield who brought flesh-and-blood back into poetry, I mean also that he has a sense of the will of man, directing the flesh-and-blood for good or evil. Kipling's verse demonstrates the activities of man as observed from a distant vantage-point; he saw man collectively, and his individuals are just one of the collection; he recognized Free Will intellectually but he did not embrace it imaginatively. That is why an element of ridicule can be detected in Kipling's attitude to man's endeavours, and as such is undoubtedly edifying. But it is a one-sided view of flesh-and-blood. The purpose Kipling recognized was the purpose of the community, and it was not even a universal community: John Masefield is nothing like so abstract; he is aware of the will of man, and can be criticized so far as he does not sufficiently recognize the will of God. Still, it is the human species he is out to represent, and the human species is very seldom conscious of the will of God. It was an exclusive sense of the will of God operating outside of man, and almost no sense of man's freedom and purpose which makes Kipling's flesh-and-blood something of a caricature.

Some of Masefield's people can also be possessed of a will outside of them, good or evil. I am thinking not only of Saul Kane in *The Everlasting Mercy*, but of the Dauber, marked as an outsider by his obsession with his art, and of the fanatical Captain Duntisbourne in the novel *Bird of Dawning*. Such characters are there because it takes all kinds to make a world; because by their rareness, they illustrate how truly flesh-and-blood are their fellow-men. But, save in the poem

Dauber, it is not Masefield's 'extraordinary' people who make the story, they only vary it. But these 'ordinary' people are not too ordinary to be true; Masefield has understood the tremendous diversity of ordinary people. No two of his characters are alike. They do extraordinary things and yet they are not extraordinary beings. Compare these fictitious people, however, with the real ones in documentary works like *Gallipoli* and *The Nine Days' Wonder*, or in an auto-biographical work like *In the Mill*, and it will be found that these are ordinary people too, doing extraordinary things. Masefield has been interested, all along, in the things of a certain magnitude done by ordinary people, and that is what he has selected from his real or imaginative experiences, to celebrate; it is just the sort of thing that will 'look well in a ballad'.

But because ordinary people are doing less and less of the extraordinary, it is improbable that there will be another poet of Masefield's kind for a very long time indeed. For this reason alone, he is important in the history of our literature. For this reason, too, it is probable that for our own time the work of his which we shall feel most sympathetic towards, is *Dauber*, the poem in which the unique man is offset against the common run of men. For the Dauber's isolation has become a universal condition – it portrays not only the soul of the artist but the soul of the sensitive man existing in a state of transition between an individualist and a regimented society. In this sense, the poem is not the most typical of Masefield's work; if we are looking for a typical poem, we must look to *Reynard the Fox*, where what I have called the poet's historical importance and where the uniqueness I have spoken of, are consummately shown.

The reasons for my own preference for *Reynard the Fox* are concerned more strictly with his literary, rather than historical importance. This poem, I believe, attains the point at which intensity of vision and artistic certainty are equally balanced, and it is a great poem. The intensity of John

Masefield's vision is manifest throughout his work; artistic certainty is another thing. Where there is, as with Masefield, a plenitude, even an over-abundance of work, we are forced to judge material which a more cautious or self-critical author would have left unpublished. With seven volumes of Wordsworth before him, Matthew Arnold marvelled that 'pieces of high merit are mingled with a mass of pieces very inferior to them'. 'It seems wonderful,' said Arnold, 'how the same poet should have produced both.' Masefield's critic is in something of this position. Masefield has never been a cautious poet. Self-critical he must be to some degree, as his writings on the nature of poetry reveal. But he has never been self-critical enough. Therefore we find, as we do with all poets who give in plenty – with Browning, with Tennyson – we find, particularly among the poems, a great many that do not come off, along with the undoubted successes. But Masefield's lapses seem to differ in kind from those of Browning or Tennyson. If *dull* verse and plain *bad* verse can be distinct, then it is dull verse that bores us in Tennyson and Browning, and it is plain bad verse that shocks us in Masefield. For the great must always be dull at times – not only did Homer nod but St Paul put a young man to sleep with one of his sermons. Dull work has its own sort of badness, but the quality of technical badness that comes sometimes from Masefield is truly incredible. And to confound us still more, this badness is often found no more than a few lines away from really fine verse. For the purpose of demonstration I take the most extreme example I can find – *No man takes the farm*:

> No man takes the farm,
> Nothing grows there;
> The ivy's arm
> Strangles the roses there.

Good, economical, and a very appropriate image of the ivy and the rose? Well, here's the next verse:

> Old Farmer Kyrle
> Farmed there the last;
> He beat his girl
> (It's seven years past).

There is worse to come. Verses seven, eight and nine, thus:

> Young Will, the son,
> Heard his sister shriek;
> He took his gun
> Quick as a streak.
>
> He said: 'Now, dad,
> Stop, once for all!'
> He was a good lad,
> Good at kicking the ball.
>
> His father clubbed
> The girl on the head.
> Young Will upped
> And shot him dead.

A bucolic farce? No, Masefield is in dead earnest. Young Will is hanged in Gloucester jail. But that's not the end. Four verses complete the poem and these are of a singular and austere beauty:

> Jane walked the wold
> Like a grey gander;
> All grown old
> She would wander.
>
> She died soon:
> At high-tide,
> At full moon,
> Jane died.

The brook chatters
As at first;
The farm it waters
Is accurst.

No man takes it
Nothing grows there;
Blood straiks it,
A ghost goes there.

^So there you are. Nor can it be said, in these cases where in the course of a single work, the very bad and the very good stand side by side, that the good compensates for the bad. They are both so alien to each other, so drawn from different reserves of consciousness, that the relationship of compensation is inapplicable. And I would still hesitate to label this dichotomous element a lapse of taste, since the attribute of taste has so often attached itself in the past to the persistently mediocre, whereas genius frequently abounds with bad taste. If the phenomenon can be explained, the cause possibly has some bearing on the quantity of the poet's output. The degree of consciousness required even for the making of merely competent verse is one which operates outside the pressure of time, as do all forms of concentrated attentiveness. In fact, when the Muse has taken occasion to desert this poet, he seems to have rushed ahead without waiting humbly for her return.

This intermittent falling-off can for the most part be located in careless rhyming, that is, rhyming which is accurate so far as it is a rhyme, but imprecise or incongruous where meaning is concerned. Palmer, his contemporary, writes:

Masefield has been attacked as a slipshod poet, for being

[1]Re-reading these verses many years later (1991) for the present edition of this book, it occurs to me that they are justified by the *genre*, which resembles the American Country Ballad (e.g. *Frankie and Johnnie*).

careless and slapdash in his diction. But the Aunt Sally stone-flingers have rather overstated their grievance. It is true that he is sometimes disconcertingly uneven, and sometimes inserts nonsensical or inept words for the mere sake of effecting a correct rhyme. But this does not occur on every page, and it is better to be like that than to be merely bloodlessly competent.[1]

This critic continues: 'Masefield does not bother himself sufficiently, and gets on with the next job.' That is the truth of the matter. John Masefield is not a reflective craftsman. No doubt he has revised his work, but without a reflective attitude. He relies on instinct which frequently leads him to do things of great skill in the way of poetic technique; but his instinct sometimes fails him badly.

Having made these observations, I feel it necessary to say that, granted the unevenness, one of the great delights of Masefield's poetry comes from the way he uses language. The vigorous sweep and naturalness strike a direct contrast to the stylization of Robert Bridges and to the 'poetic' poetry of the nineties; and make small matter indeed of the Georgians, stylized as they too were, in their quasi-natural, Housmanesque manner. Such conversational ease in poetry had not appeared before Masefield since Arthur Hugh Clough – that most neglected and rare of nineteenth-century poets. Anyone who can enjoy as poetry the language of *Amours de Voyage* and *The Bothie* will find the same satisfying effortless style (though not the sophisticated tone) in John Masefield. I do not mean the rhetorical parts of Masefield's poetry (nor of Clough's) – they are there for another purpose. But in the substantial functionary parts of any of the narrative poems and in the shorter pieces too, the idiom has the same relation to common speech in Masefield's time as Clough's idiom had to the common speech of his day.[2]

[1] *Post-Victorian Poetry.*
[2] I now (1991) consider Clough's diction, in *Amours de Voyage*, at least equal to the common speech of our day.

This naturalness was not easily acquired by John Masefield. It grew from experiments in prose, much influenced by Yeats and Synge; from the experiments in verse – the closest Masefield has come to Kipling – in *Salt Water Ballads*. It finds full expression in such narrative poems as *The Everlasting Mercy, Dauber*, and *Reynard the Fox*. His prose style has developed in quite a different way; not vigour, but patience, precision, grace, inform the prose of his later novels and essays. The vigour of the poems and the 'sweetness and light' of the prose seem to me to meet in *Reynard the Fox*. *Dauber* is perhaps the most dramatically penetrating of the narrative poems; but *Reynard* is the most technically accomplished, the widest in range of characterization and action.

I have been speaking mainly of the narrative poems because I see him first as a narrative poet. But to speak of these is to represent only one of the numerous branches of Masefield's genius. There are to be considered his prolific writings about the sea, about seamen and practical seamanship, ships and voyages. In a later chapter I will devote some time to considering his vision of the sea, how vivid it is in every detail, how objective and yet how passionate. And we shall have to consider his pictorial sense and how skilfully he paints a landscape; also his historical sense and his talent for bringing the past to the present. Therefore, when we have said that John Masefield has advanced his art as a story-teller, as a portrayer of humankind, and as one who has developed the language of poetry, there is a great deal left unsaid.

You cannot get an idea of his mind only from his poems, you must also know his novels; nor from his book on Shakespeare – you must know his essay *On Rigging Model Ships* as well. His work on Rossetti reveals one aspect of him; his history of the training-ship *Conway*, another; his anthologies yet another. He has translated poems from the Spanish; he has translated Racine. He has described himself, as we have seen, 'not as a learned man', and yet his capacity for knowledge about life, in no way a superficial knowledge, is truly amazing, and is combined with a far-reaching experience of literature. I would not have it thought that, because I have narrowed the limits of this study to one aspect of Masefield – the most important aspect – I do not value the others. Indeed, I believe that all these activities of his mind are, in a sense, part of John Masefield, the supreme story-teller.

I suggested earlier that Masefield's work is not of the kind which should affect us as an interpretation of the author's life. Some types of writing, the more subjective types, call for a search for their original meaning in the personal aspects of the author's life. Masefield's work is not, in this sense, a projection of himself. It would not, for example, reward us to seek for the origins of the people who appear in *Reynard the Fox*: these people are self-explanatory. But we shall appreciate the poem better if we have read Masefield's essay on fox-hunting, and if we know that his imagination has been involved in that activity since childhood.

Where a knowledge of John Masefield's experience of life can enrich our experience of his work, is perfectly displayed in the poet's autobiographical writings. There he speaks of the friendships, the events, the places and books which matter to him imaginatively, and which formed his attitude to life. It is not a complex attitude but it is at once a broad and a sensitive one.

Two

The Man and the Vision

I

It is often remarked that Masefield is 'reticent' about himself and his own activities; and this, from frequent repetition, has become a sort of legend, as though it were an odd thing for people to keep their peace about their private affairs.

But in fact, Masefield has written more about his own life than most living authors. His autobiographies are among his best work, and many essays and reminiscences in his prose collections testify to the poet's rich and varied life. Beside *New Chum*, the story of his first term on the training-ship *Conway*, and *In the Mill*, an account of his experience as a hand in an American carpet factory, there is the long poem *Wonderings* in which his early childhood impressions are related; there are portraits of his Bloomsbury days in the early days of the century, and of his friends Yeats and Synge; and as a guide to the things, the scenes, the events which have touched the poet's imagination most lastingly, there is the poem *Biography*.[1]

It is true that a poem by Masefield calls a curse on the head of his future biographer. 'Print not my life nor letters, put them by,' writes the poet, 'when I am dead let memory of me die. . . .' But Masefield has made lavish provision for

[1] A third autobiographical book *So Long to Learn*, covering these and other periods of the poet's life, appeared in 1952. *Grace Before Ploughing: Fragments of an Autobiography* was published in 1966.

those who find interesting in his life what he himself has found most interesting, and what has influenced him as a poet and a story-teller. So that, while the biographer will be courageous who prints Masefield's life and letters, the critic who neglected Masefield's autobiographies would be idle.

What is of importance to the recorder of those aspects of the man that tally with the vision expressed in his work, is the poem *Biography*, because it is addressed precisely to the 'penman' of Masefield's life story. He contemplates the time when

> . . . all my thoughts and acts
> Will be reduced to lists of dates and facts.

and the day when

> . . . men will call the golden hour of bliss
> 'About this time' or 'shortly after this'.

The poet goes on to describe what are the genuine 'facts' of his history: 'golden instants and bright days' which make up the sum of experience far beyond the power of such facts as one might find, perhaps, in *Who's Who*. The significant things in his life, he is telling us here, are things for which there is no apparent result to show. The ships he saw and sailed in, the friends of the sea days and the friends of the Bloomsbury days, the 'windy gas-lamps and the wet roads shining', 'St Pancras' bells striking two'; 'wild days in a pamero off the Plate'; 'Hills and great waters'; a June day

> . . . when, in the red bricks' chinks,
> I saw the old Roman ruins white with pinks,
> And felt the hillside haunted even then
> By not dead memory of the Roman men.

In fragments of circumstance such as these, in such intense

and 'glittering moments', the poet's experience has been crystallized.

These are the experiences which matter to him, because they have affected his imagination. It would be sentimentally inaccurate to oppose the more renowned and outward events of his life to the spirit of the poem *Biography* and pretend they do not matter; his appointment as Poet Laureate and the academic and civic honours conferred upon him have their own sort of importance, and must undoubtedly have influenced the poet's development.

But we are concerned, in this chapter, to discover the vision in the man and the man in the vision; and these things were there, potentially, from the start – long before the memorable week when the publication of *The Everlasting Mercy* made John Masefield the most widely-read poet since Kipling.

His imagination – that is really our subject. John Masefield's imagination manifests itself in the portrayal of action, though, as we see in the poem *Biography*, it draws on a complex mosaic of images. And whereas, in fact, the poet now lives a studious, retired life, he has the unusual knack of participating, imaginatively, in the doings of his fellow-men. The partial detachment from life required of every writer, and especially one of Masefield's prodigious output, seems to have increased his capacity for experience: in most poets, it is a capacity for reflection which develops with the exercise of their art. Masefield's readers are bound to wonder at the sheer range of human activities in which so industrious a writer finds time to take so concentrated an interest.

In this age, the serious creative writer who is at the same time capable of self-identification with the activities (as apart from the impulses, desires, motives) of his fellow-men, is phenomenal. The full current of life, the exhilaration of action, has never been very strong in literary people, though they have often liked to believe so. Masefield is at once an object of curiosity and awe, in his happy facility for counting nothing alien to him which concerns mankind. It is truly amazing that nothing whatever seems to bore him.

II
'The Ledbury Scene'

John Masefield was born 'in or near' Ledbury in Hereford-shire, as he tells us, 'on or nearly on' 1 June, 1878.[1]

His childhood, as it emerges from his accounts of it, follows the familiar pattern of Victorian middle-class life in rural England. To compensate for the number of 'forbidden' activities, there was a capacious environment, range of movement, and, perhaps in consequence, range of imagin-ation, denied to the middle-class juvenile to-day.

Whenever the poet writes of his childhood, his thoughts seem to dwell on the idea of wonder. (Indeed, *Wonderings* is the title he gives to the verse-reminiscence of his childhood.) Of his early years, Masefield invariably speaks with a kind of respect, which arises partly from his recognition of this sense of wonder he was endowed with, from earliest infancy. And he recognizes, too, how powerful an influence his early environment, his childhood readings and imaginings, have had on his life and destiny as a poet. He tells us, '. . . when, after much vain effort, I began to write, the scenes of my tales were those familiar to my childhood.'[2] In this specific sense, the Ledbury countryside has direct bearing on much that Masefield has written, and in fact on his best work.

Orphaned, and brought up by relatives in an old rambling house with a 'big straggly garden', John Masefield tells of the two things most important to him: his grandfather's library, and, just beyond the garden, the churchyard and church of Ledbury.

'I was ever a greedy reader,' he writes in a reminiscence of

[1] *So Long to Learn.*
[2] *St. Katherine of Ledbury* (1951).

25

this period. Whatever the books were – bound volumes of monthly magazines and others 'dealing mostly with antiquities' – he seized on them and if these contained stories, so much the better. 'Stories of some kind,' he writes, 'were going on in my head whenever I was alone; three or four main stories (none about myself) going from incident to incident and climate to climate.'[1] The fact that none of these stories was about himself is unusual. Most children, when they invent stories, place themselves in the centre of the action; and I think this shows that John Masefield's remarkable sense of objectivity was there from the start.

His reading was varied. In *Chamber's Journal* he discovered Red Indians; in the back Christmas numbers of magazines he found ghost stories which he 'read with zest and full belief; at any rate till nearly sunset'. Other books which he got hold of were of a loftier nature: Lord Chesterfield's *Letters to His Son*, the novels of Fielding, the *Fables* of Gay.

'It was thought (he writes) that I was too much given to reading. Surely anything that takes a child's mind from the horrors of daily life to horrors that are over or only imagined cannot be altogether wrong.'[2] Not, perhaps, an unanswerable argument: but the poet's is a particular case. 'In my case, stories were necessary; to me most other studies seemed tame or foolish. . . .'

Discouragement seems merely to have given edge to his persistence in the consuming of stories. And can we doubt that discouragement whetted his resolve to be a story-teller? When, as a boy on the training-ship *Conway* he indulged in speculations about his future, it was said 'What? You a writer? How can you be a writer? Only clever people are writers: and terrible lives they lead, both in this world and the next.'[3]

Along with his reading, the poet rates the church of

[1] *So Long to Learn.*
[2] *Ibid.*
[3] *Ibid.*

26

Ledbury as a place meaningful to his early years. Sunday morning service was no less an agony to him than it was to thousands of Victorian children, but attached to the church were several compensating 'attractions', made more attractive, no doubt, by the fact that they were erratic in appearance. Such marvels as a Church Parade with band, and the unexpected appearance of birds in the church, are counted as attractions, although, as the poet remarks, 'There were more services than attractions.'

One attraction which he was never to forget was that provided by the church bells, of which he writes: 'At every third hour they chimed Bishop Heber's hymn, "Holy, holy, holy" to Dykes' *Nicæa*, with effects of enchantment,' reminding us inevitably of the lines from *The Everlasting Mercy*.

> The clocks struck three, and sweetly, slowly,
> The bells chimed Holy, Holy, Holy;

Quite recently, hearing that the Ledbury bells had been silenced for want of costly repair, John Masefield wrote his booklet *St Katherine of Ledbury* to benefit a fund set up for the purpose. 'It is not easy,' he writes, 'to describe the pang that I felt, when I heard that the bells had to be silenced.'

Sometimes John Masefield would find the door of the bell-tower open and climb up to the belfry which provided a good hiding-place. From this point he could 'climb out on to the leads, and look upward at the spire, to the golden Bird of Paradise forty yards above me. . . .'

This golden, paradisal Bird is referred to again in *Wonderings*:

> Life's other glory topped the church's spire,
> A golden vane surveying half the shire,
> A weather-cock serene in the assails
> Of tree-upsetting, ship-destroying gales.
> Pinnacled, plumey, lonely, there he shone,
> Swinging to shifts, but never moving on,

Braving, perhaps, the blasts that were to be
Death to the *Captain* and *Eurydice*.
Lofty as any clipper's skysail truck,
Steadfast as life, as certainless as luck,
Seeing him swinging to the wester's drive
I ever thought that golden bird alive.

And surely it is this Bird which appears in *The Everlasting Mercy* as the 'glittering peacock' whose crowing demolishes the churchyard ghosts. It is certainly the church of Ledbury, with its early Gothic work, which is filled with the ghostly congregation, appearing so unexpectedly in this realistic poem:

> All the old monks' singing places
> Glimmered quick with flitting faces,
> Singing anthems, singing hymns
> Under carven cherubims.

The phantom choir itself dates from the poet's earliest imaginings. 'I was told,' he writes, 'that the church had been a Collegiate Church, served by a College of Priests . . . The idea of a religious community there, getting up at midnight to sing, never failed to thrill me.'[1]

The poet's childhood impressions of Ledbury are intimately associated with *The Everlasting Mercy* in many other respects. The story itself is partly based on a Ledbury tale about two poachers who fought for the right to poach some of the coverts. Masefield dates this fight about the mid-1850s. It is not a great deal to base a story on, but a little goes a long way with a born story-teller. 'When I wrote my verses,' Masefield tells us, 'it was from memory of what existed or perhaps I imagined to exist, when I was a child.'[2] Thus, he is able to draw on these piercing memories, even now, to give the exact topography of the poem, though sometimes his

[1] *So Long to Learn.*
[2] *St. Katherine of Ledbury.*

28

memory and the Ordnance Survey Map of 1931 are at variance when he compares them. 'I put,' he begins, 'the scene of the challenge and the fight on the open, somewhat barren pasture above Coneygree Wood on the field-track leading to Eastnor Knoll and Eastnor. The Map of 1931 calls this expanse The Golf Course.' The opening scene of the story,

> By Dead Man's Thorn, while setting wires . . .

turns out to be Dead Woman's Thorn by the map. 'This may be the right name,' Masefield remarks, 'but it is new to myself.'[1]

Many are the actual places in and around Ledbury celebrated in *The Everlasting Mercy*, *The Widow in the Bye Street*, *The Daffodil Fields*, *Reynard the Fox* and other poems. Indeed, anyone moved to exhaustively explore 'The Masefield Country' with his Collected Works bulging in their pockets could not do better than consult the last chapter of *St Katherine of Ledbury* where the poet gives topographical details in abundance.

The poem *Wonderings* is perhaps the best guide to the poet's early impressions. In the margin is printed, eighteenth-century style, the progressive 'items' of the poem. Those wonders of the world which, in the poet's memory, most profoundly impressed him as a child, include such items as 'Delight in Water', 'Claver Cope', 'The Flowers', 'The Town', 'Timber Waggons' of which a sample:

> . . . daily up the Bye Street timber-waggons
> Dragged the chained scaly butts like slaughtered
>   dragons.
> It was delight to see those timber-teams
> The iron of their shag-hoofs striking gleams,
> Their brasses bright, their mighty crests at strain,

[1] *St Katherine of Ledbury.*

With crack of whip-shot coming up the lane,
And where the narrow lane-end opened wide
The corded carter ran ahead to guide

The list embraces also 'The Old Canal' and 'The Barges':

The barges were blunt-ended tanks,
With rub-strakes polished by the banks,
And bearing dingy freight for fee,
But, oh, when, just beneath my eyes
The dreadful eddies made them rise,
When, within touch, I looked into
The darling cabin of the crew
The little house with bunks and stove
For her who steered and him who drove. . . .

Then there are such joys remembered in remarkably vivid
detail, as 'The Western View' which reached as far as the
Welsh Black Mountains, beyond Wye. There are 'The
Bargeman's Inns' which were 'kept by the Seven Deadly
Sins', though the poet asserts that he never saw

The seven breakers of the law,
Only their washing hung from lines
And dingy, painted, swinging signs,
And empty alleys with none stirring
Save possibly a black cat purring,
Doubtless a cat with Satan's mark
Who rode a broomstick after dark.

Those who were nurtured on Masefield's fantasy of childhood, *The Midnight Folk*, are sure to recognize this marvellous
Cat, and will certainly find a trace of the fancy-filled and
lonely young hero in the poet's account of his own bed-time
thoughts:

Ah, after dark, when bound for bed,
What images were in my head

Of lamplight in those secret houses
And songs and fiddles and carouses
And ear-ringed bargemen sipping rum
Defying death and kingdom come,
Telling the marvels of the seas
From Maelstrom to the Ramireez.
For who could doubt those swarthy men
Knew Tenedos and Darien,

There is one other note in John Masefield's early childhood that should be recorded here, as it marks the awakening of an interest which culminated in his finest work, *Reynard the Fox*.

In an introduction to an American edition of the poem[1] he writes: 'Once, when I was, perhaps, five years old, the fox was hunted into our garden, and those glorious beings in scarlet, as well as the hounds, were all about my lairs, like visitants from Paradise. The fox, on this occasion, went through a woodshed and escaped.'

'Hounds and hunting filled my imagination,' writes the poet. Hunting was, in fact, the staple interest of that countryside in his young days, and though John Masefield followed many a hunt, he remembers each one, its 'colour and intensity of beauty'. Even in those days he had conceived an admiration for the fox. This attitude was never sentimentalized; it did not stop him hunting; and this outright appreciation of the visual beauty of the meet, the beauty of the chase, the grace and skill of the fox whose movement the poet describes as a 'leisurely hurry' – this direct, clear, sensual savouring, is one of the highly success-ful qualities of the poem. 'No fox was the original of my Reynard,' he writes, 'but as I was much in the woods as a boy, I saw foxes fairly often, considering that they are night-moving animals. Their grace, beauty, cleverness and secrecy always thrilled me.'

The Herefordshire scene appears and reappears through-

[1] Reprinted as *Foxhunting* (*Recent Prose* 1926).

out Masefield's work. In most of his novels, some part of that countryside can be discerned, and, in his sea stories, should some English sailor be made to think or speak of his home, it is usually located in the West Midlands.

When, in October 1930, Masefield was given the Freedom of the City of Hereford, he declared, 'I am linked to this County by subtle ties, deeper than I can explain: they are ties of beauty. . . . I know no land more full of bounty and beauty than this red land, so good for corn and hops and roses. . . .'

III
The Conway

In September 1891, aged thirteen, John Masefield left the red ploughlands, the rivers, the woods, the meadows and the little town with its ancient church; he left his childhood behind and set off to become a trainee, traditionally known as a 'new chum' on H.M.S. *Conway*, a training-ship in the Mersey. 'Expectation,' says Masefield 'was lively in me; as someone says of Shakespeare, "he had the Phantsie very strong".' Most of this expectation rested on the forthcoming hammock, sea-chest and other items of equipment which were to be his. The first night aboard someone unhooked the New Chum's hammock. Hammock and the future Poet Laureate landed on the deck.

New Chum (1944) tells in the poet's delightful, autobiographical style, of his first term on the *Conway*. Here he learned the rudiments of sailing ships and also, to some extent, of people. To the ship's life he brought an eager questioning spirit. True, the questions that presented themselves to him were not always on the most lofty level. It was a matter of some internal debate, for instance, whether it would be fatal if one contracted a blood poisoning from sitting on a bent pin, carefully arranged by a fellow Chum, and if so, would a death thus induced during Divine Service count as martyrdom?

On the *Conway* John Masefield got himself a reputation as a story-teller and picked up not a few hints in the art from older hands. The hardships, new to him, were compensated for by practically everything else that was new to him. He felt both fascinated and bewildered by this 'cramped odd life between decks, this smell of paint and tar, this rush, tumult and order, an utter absence of privacy of any kind. . . .'

Solitude he found at last in a place he loved for its own sake: 'I went up to the cross-trees, and again marvelled at the miracle of what I saw; a River full of ships of all sorts; two cities full of ships of all sorts; and far away mountains, blue and gold.' In those solitary moments aloft the panorama of sea-life began to display itself before him as he has since revealed it to others. He went aloft whenever he got the chance, and never failed to be stirred by the beauty of the river.

It was on the *Conway* that Masefield acquired a copy of *Treasure Island*. 'I started reading it there and then,' he says, 'with the feeling that it had been written for me, and that no boy in the wide world could be enjoying it as I did. All the characters were on board with me. Long John Silver, though with two legs and without any parrot, was in the port fore. Billy Bones and old Pew were in the port main. Merry was in the fourth class with me. All our officers were touched off to the life. . . .'

But there was little time for reading in this first term, and many exciting distractions. The absorption with which young John Masefield would gaze at the shipping which came and went, taught him how to appreciate and judge, and how to describe a ship. 'I was beyond all mortals lucky in seeing and knowing something of those decades of the sailing ship, the three in which she touched perfection, as man-of-war, as bird of passage, and as carrier.'

It was on the *Conway* that Masefield first heard of the glories of 'the clipper ship, the Australian voyage and the Tea Race from the Min River', embodied in his novel, *Bird of*

Dawning. From the decks of the *Conway* he first saw the *Wanderer*. Himself a wanderer, the poet seems to feel a special impulse of tenderness and pride towards the tragic *Wanderer*. His book *The Wanderer of Liverpool* (1930), gives the entire and noble history of this remarkable ship. 'The *Wanderer* with great beauty and strange dooms' he described it in the poem *Ships*, and in *Biography*, is noted:

> The glittering day when all the waves wore flags
> And the ship *Wanderer* came with sails in rags;

Judging from the reproductions of paintings and photographs which appear in *The Wanderer of Liverpool*, she was all that is claimed for her when John Masefield first saw her from the *Conway* in the autumn of 1891. The *Wanderer* appears to have remained a symbol to the poet ever since: a symbol of grace and power and nobility of effort in spite of failure. This was the first great ship he had ever seen, and one of the most significant passages in *New Chum* records his first sight of the ship which was to mean so much to him. 'I liked the name, the *Wanderer*. It stuck into my mind as a name of beauty, as a sort of seagull of grace there. The *Wanderer* . . . the more I thought of the name, the more wonderful it seemed. It suggested skies of desolation, with a planet; seas of loneliness, with that ship in sail. She was to sail soon, they said. . . .'

After a week she sailed, into bad weather. Within a week she returned 'The *Wanderer* came out of the greyness into sunlight as a thing of such beauty as the world can seldom show. . . . She had been lopped at all her cross-trees, and the wreck of her upper spans was lashed in her lower rigging. As she turned, her tattered sails (nearly all were tattered), suddenly shone all over her; her beautiful sheer, with its painted ports, shone. I had seen nothing like her in all my life. . . .'

It will be observed, time and again in the poet's writings,

how invariably he finds an exalted beauty in the symbol of great, though defeated, endeavour.

IV
Apprentice Poet

While still in his teens John Masefield became a deep-sea deck-hand, a pot-boy in a New York bar, a farm-hand, a worker in an American carpet factory and an ardent reader of English literature. Before he was twenty, he had also conceived a longing to be a writer, 'but this longing was very deeply buried, under the more immediate longing to read and read. . . .'[1]

It may have been from the unconscious motive of preserving himself as an artist that John Masefield decided not to make the sea his career, much though he loved it. The same sort of questions that arise in his poem *Dauber* may have occurred to him at this time, and indeed, as he has written of himself in those days when he was wondering whether to continue as a sailor, the vocation seemed to him 'a grand life, no one could deny that; but if you want to read and read, it was the wrong life'.

The decision to give up the sea was eminently sound. It could not have been an easy one to reach. John Masefield knew the sea well. He knew what to expect from life at sea, even during good weather. 'Any leisure,' he writes, 'used for study was taken from necessary sleep, and then with every conceivable disadvantage which the public life of the sea entails. Then, at sea, in addition to the hardness of the work at all times and the hardships of cold and wet, one suffered from the semi-starvation of the lime-juicer's allowance, which was much the kind of food given to the ordinary dog, but markedly worse than that given to the hound. The

[1] *In the Mill* (1941).

35

hound has boiled horse. God knows what it was that the seaman had.'[1]

Against these hardships, multiplied many times, John Masefield had to weigh his great love for the sea. In a few years it had altogether got into his blood, and in the midst of the greatest danger and suffering he had gained many an experience of unforgettable intensity. His poems and fiction are full of scenes which combine the horror and the beauty of life on a sailing vessel. And often he speaks directly of a personal experience. On one such occasion he writes, introducing a 'strangely beautiful shanty . . . known as Hanging Johnny. It has a melancholy tune that is one of the saddest things I have ever heard. I heard it for the first time off the Horn, in a snowstorm, when we were hoisting topsails after heavy weather. There was a heavy grey sea running and the decks were awash. The skies were sodden and oily, shutting in the sea about a quarter of a mile away. . . . I cannot repeat those words to their melancholy wavering music without seeing the line of yellow oilskins, the wet deck, the frozen ropes, and the great grey seas running up into the sky.'[2]

Either directly, or through the characters in his novels and poems, Masefield insists on the memorable beauty of sea life. The beauty of changing weather, the beauty of companionship, of skill in seamanship, of the strange, the incredible sailors' stories and the beauty of the mythology of the sea – this John Masefield missed whenever he took jobs ashore. 'I missed very much the link of the ship; no man can fail to feel for a ship as for a living thing. . . . Then, she is always a beautiful thing, usually in my time, a superlatively lovely thing exquisite to see. . . .'[3]

It is always remarkable, the degree of detachment the poet seems to have been able to bring to the most difficult and

---

[1] *In the Mill*
[2] Quoted in *John Masefield: A study,* by Cecil Biggane (1924).
[3] *In the Mill.*

rigorous situations. It *seems* so, because, when he comes to recount his adventures, he always gives calm evidence. There is never any hint of personal resentment against the world. Though he constantly denounces stupidity, particularly in those in power, he is able to say, looking back at a time of hardship and depression during the 'nineties in New York, 'Depressions seemed to me a part of life, to be expected like snowstorms or frosts or fog.'

This is characteristic of John Masefield. His early book of essays and memories, *A Tarpaulin Muster*, tells with that intense interest in the phenomenon of which he writes – to the total exclusion of any selfward emotion – how he was almost arrested for selling liquor out of hours when he was a pot-boy in a New York saloon. Of himself, Masefield merely observes that he 'had a good opportunity of noting how a law might be evaded'. Fortunately, the arrest did not come off. The scene closes with the young bartender serving champagne and cucumber sandwiches to his employer and two detectives: 'I put down the wine and poured out three creaming glasses. "Here's happy days," said the boss. "Drink hearty," said one detective. "Let her go, boys," said the other. "Fill them up again," said the boss. "You may go now, John," he added.'[1]

In a carpet factory John Masefield gained not only a good skill at handling the looms but a new experience of companionship among the workers. What concerns us most in his story (*In the Mill*) of this phase of his career, however, is the account of the poet's intellectual awakening. He read Malory, and noted that Tennyson seemed lifeless beside him. Herman Melville's *The Green Hand* he had read but it 'was not much use to me' – a phrase which suggests that already he was reading as a writer reads, with a view to using the book for his own development. He read other works by Melville, and enjoyed parts of *Moby Dick*. Surprisingly, he

[1] *A Tarpaulin Muster* (1907).

does not seem to have been an enthusiast for Melville at this time, though he was keenly interested in all sea literature.

One book, however, stimulated the poet beyond all others; it became, in a way, a key to the rest of his reading for some time to come. This was George du Maurier's *Trilby*. It was not so much the work itself – though John Masefield enjoyed it more than any book he had read until then – which played so prominent a part in forming his tastes, but the other works which George du Maurier put John Masefield on to, through *Trilby*. For instance, 'It gave me,' writes the poet, '. . . an impression of France which I have never lost, and quoted to me, for the first time, scraps of French verse which seemed very beautiful. I told myself, that I was indeed ignorant, that I knew nothing of English and less than nothing of French. . . .'[1]

Whatever book *Trilby* mentions, John Masefield bought. He also bought a French grammar. On the oblique recommendations in *Trilby* he read the *Three Musketeers*; Sterne's *Sentimental Journey*; Darwin's *Origin of the Species*.

After *Trilby* came the effect of *Peter Ibbetson*. 'It came to me,' writes the poet of this book, 'just when I most needed an inner life.' From *Peter Ibbetson* he learned of the existence of Villon and of de Musset. He read these poets but 'the time was not ripe for either'.

The ways in which those who seek, find, have often a curious aspect of accident: certain phrases by literary journalists stuck in John Masefield's memory – 'had I the pen of de Quincey' or 'had I the opium-tinted imagination of de Quincey'; the young poet began to wonder 'who was this de Quincey, and what sort of a pen had he?' From *The Confessions of an Opium Eater* he discovered Wordsworth.

The essays of Steele and Addison, whose prose has so greatly influenced his own, seem to have impressed but, at this time, not moved him. Likewise, Pope, whose translation

[1] *In the Mill.*

of the *Odyssey* found the young reader 'by no means skilled enough to perceive the perfection of much of the verse' – 'But I found the story worth the trouble,' Masefield adds.

The haphazard selection of books the poet mentions having read at this time shows an instinct for his needs as a writer. He needed to dip and taste and savour. He needed knowledge of different literary cultures. These books were like unpieced parts of a mosaic, which later was to take shape in his mind.

The instinct which prevented the poet from dedicating his life to the sea intervened once more when he seriously considered studying for the medical profession to which he was greatly drawn. At this point he acquired a volume of Keats and one of Shelley. He began with Keats: 'I was in a world where incredible beauty was daily bread and breath of life. Everything that I had read until then seemed like paving-stones on the path leading to this Paradise; . . . I knew, then, that life is very brief, and that the use of life is to discover the law of one's being, and to follow that law, at whatever cost, to the utmost. I knew then that Medicine was not the law of my being, but the shadow of it, and that my law was to follow poetry. . . .'[1]

To consider the implications of his response to Shelley will perhaps help to place the growth of Masefield's poetic sensibility against its historical background. 'On first reading Shelley,' he writes, 'I told myself that this was a new kind of verse, such as I had not known existed.' Now it was the *verse*, not the argument, which had an effect upon Masefield, which he describes as 'electric and ecstatic', and he tells how excited he was by the *construction* of the *Revolt of Islam*. This is worth remembering, now that we are inclined to underrate Shelley's technical achievement and concentrate with approval or otherwise on his 'philosophy'.

Before John Masefield sailed for England, working his

[1] *In the Mill.*

passage, in the year of Queen Victoria's Diamond Jubilee, he had come to a first acquaintanceship with Chaucer to whom he has been so often compared; and in spite of the difficulties of language, the young poet saw that he was dealing with 'a lively spirit, providing good entertainment for all hands'. Before his departure for his native land he had read some of Dickens and Stevenson; more important to him, Swinburne (whom presently he was to see plain), Rossetti and William Morris. John Masefield's debt to William Morris as a constructive thinker is considerable. It may be that William Morris has been the formative influence, in his limitations as well as his liberations, on Masefield's view of life. Masefield writes of him always with reverence, and I think the voice of Morris is never very far off when Masefield propounds a social theory through the characters in his books.

He had begun to practise his art before leaving America. He experimented much in verse. Of course he had started a novel 'and wished that the dull parts might get done, so that I could get my heroine aboard the lugger, whose saucy decks, alas, she never trod.'

He had a longing for London, a need to associate himself with the literary movements of the time, and to take his chance as a writer. One of his companions in the carpet factory advised him earnestly against such a hazardous course. 'He said at once "O, no, John; I wouldn't do that. You've got no job to go to there. You have a good job here. If you stay on, why, you'll very likely have a section before long; and after that, you might even come to have a floor."'

V

Bloomsbury Days

In his poem *Biography* Masefield speaks of 'years blank with hardship'. Slowly the new poet made his way to London.

Illness overtook him and he was not expected to live. 'Blank with hardship' though these years were, the poet was soon to find a place among others of his own kind, new and stimulating friendships were to be formed of lifelong importance to the poet. Life was not all blankness.

> So, if the penman sums my London days,
> Let him but say that there were holy ways.

In an article in *The Atlantic Monthly* he tells a little of what he was reading at this time, and who were the writers most influential to his work. 'My masters ... in poetry, were Swinburne and Meredith among the living, Rossetti, Matthew Arnold and Robert Browning among the lately dead. To these I would add Edward Fitzgerald. . . . In prose, the masters were Stendhal, Flaubert, Villiers de l'Isle-Adam, Guy de Maupassant, Prosper Mérimée and Walter Pater.'[1]

It was a time of flux and influx. Fine writing and realism were what John Masefield was after in prose. In poetry, it was the upsurge of feeling and rhythm first released by Swinburne. Masefield wrote in a letter to me after my first meeting with him, 'Swinburne meant much to my generation: he was literary: he adored the French masters, who were then our masters in all things: he was generous beyond most poets, in his praise and likings: he was one of the real discoverers of Blake: he could write exquisite verse in an age of exquisite verse: he laid us all at his feet with half a dozen things which I cannot read without emotion now. He was one of the first romantic modern poets to be read by me: and *Chastelard*, to a boy, is all that the heart can desire and the lines on the death of Baudelaire all that genius and grief can utter.'[2]

Pondering over illuminated manuscripts, books and

[1]Reprinted in *So Long to Learn*.
[2]Letter to the author dated Dec. 1950.

magazines in museums and libraries, Masefield was already
a well-read man when, at the age of twenty-one, he came
across the works of Yeats, whose disciple he became and
whom he shortly met.

Masefield has written of Yeats, always with warmth,
admiration and delight. In *Biography* he tells of

> . . . that old room (above the noisy slum),
> Where there was wine and fire and talk with some
> Under strange pictures of the wakened soul
> To whom this earth was but a burnt-out coal.

In *A Book of Both Sorts* he has described that 'old room above
the noisy slum', in close and fascinating detail. Yeats' room
on the second floor of Number 18, Woburn Buildings, was,
Masefield tells us – and who could doubt it? – 'the most
interesting room in London at that time'.

Masefield has his own way of describing this room. It
consists of telling the reader what objects were in the room,
and allowing the list to have a cumulative effect. The result
is, that in a very short space is given one of the most vivid
accounts in existence of the sort of environment Yeats
created for himself. (Very frequently, when describing
something, Masefield employs a nautical image; here, too,
he indulges the pleasant habit):

> After 1904–5, [Yeats] added to the room a big dark-blue lectern,
> on which his Kelmscott Chaucer stood, between enormous
> candles in big blue wooden sconces. These candles, when new,
> stood four feet high, and were as thick as a ship's oar.[1]

Yeats had a pencil drawing by Cecil French 'of a woman
holding a rose in her lips'. In this essay, Masefield remarks
on the beauty of the drawing, and surely he had this
Carmenesque portrait in mind when he wrote of the dancer
with the flower between her lips in his novel *The Square Peg*.

[1] *W.B. Yeats (A Book of Both Sorts* 1947).

Of Yeats himself, Masefield has written always with affectionate insight, recording those outward characteristics of the older poet which seem to give us an immediate clue to his personality:

> When greeting or parting with a friend, he stood very erect and lifted his right hand above his head. This gesture of his he kept until the last time I saw him. It was a strangely beautiful gesture; the man himself; unearthly and beautiful, with a winning and witty charm unequalled in our time.[1]

Those evenings in company with Yeats and his friends are celebrated again in *Biography*:

> Those friends who heard St. Pancras's bells strike two
> Yet stayed until the barber's cockerel crew,
> Talking of noble styles. . . .

It was at one of Yeats' Monday evenings that John Masefield met John Synge. 'My host introduced me, with the remark that he wanted us to know each other,'[2] Masefield writes in his essay on Synge. They became friends. Synge, reserved and uncommunicative, is described as 'a perfect companion'.

That Synge was interested in life itself, and not mere commentary on life, is a fact on which Masefield insists repeatedly. '[Synge] was puzzled by the talk of the clever young men from Oxford. "That's a queer way to talk. They all talk like that. I wonder what makes them talk like that? I suppose they're always stewing over dead things."'

Synge, as Masefield remembers him, was known as a 'natural' writer (as compared with a 'literary' man). He tells us that Synge composed his plays straight on to the typewriter. He must have been one of the first creative writers to do so.

---

[1] *A Book of Both Sorts.*
[2] *John M. Synge (Recent Prose* 1932).

The sort of thing John Masefield remembers about Yeats is rather different from his memory of Synge. With Yeats, it is the gesture, the idiosyncratic furnishings of his room, the peculiar way he chanted his verse. The recollections of Synge are scenic: the time Synge watched an egg being boiled in a paper box, keenly interested, and afterwards examining the box; the hours spent in Synge's company at a then humble Restaurant des Gourmets. 'We spent happy hours there,' Masefield writes, 'talking, rolling cigarettes, and watching the life.'

From Yeats' Monday evenings the two friends would walk home together, John Synge and John Masefield.

> Often at night I tread those streets again,
> . . . .
> And now I miss that friend who used to walk
> Home to my lodgings with me, deep in talk,
> Wearing the last of night out in still streets
> . . . Now I miss
> That lively mind and guttural laugh of his,

I do not think it is too much to say that these two friendships altered the whole course of John Masefield's career. The opportunity to exchange views with those whose lives were wholly occupied with literature was necessary and important to him. And the actual influence they exerted on his work is very strong; it was not always and entirely a favourable influence (for the greatest writers are not necessarily the best mentors); still, when a writer is beginning, any guide – even one who leads him off his course – may serve to get him going.

Masefield feels, himself, that he did not really start writing until 1911, with *The Everlasting Mercy*. On the whole, I think he is right, and it is difficult to identify the author of the narrative poems from 1911 onwards with the disciple of early Yeats and of Synge, or with the avowed Pre-Raphaelite, the follower of Rossetti, 'touched by a twilight of romance from France' – and we must look in the earlier work for signs of these formative years when, as the poet puts it, 'all literature was seething around us in a fervour of energy undreamed of to-day', and at a time when, he reminds us, 'we had in full fervour the Imperialist movement, the art for art's sake opposition, the Celtic Renascence, studies from over the seas, a French school, a Kail-yard school, a native product of romance and of sport, and a gifted decadence.'[1]

Before the poet went to live at Great Hampden, where he wrote *The Everlasting Mercy*, he had met many prominent literary men of his time, and had published more work than many authors produce in a lifetime. He had also worked on the staff of the *Manchester Guardian*.

VI
A Reflective Phase: The Sonnets

By 1911, the poet had discovered himself. He had become stabilized and even without the tremendous success of *The Everlasting Mercy*, the recognition of John Masefield as a writer of distinction and individuality, was imminent.

Masefield's imaginative development begins to take on another pattern from this point. Where before his mind was taking root – absorbing the elements necessary to his progress, from books, friends and daily life – he now seems to develop through his own work. In the narrative verse the process appears to be a technical one; but his sonnet sequence (contained in *Lollingdon Downs*), published in 1916, consummates a need for philosophical formulation.

The poet was now in a postion to produce the first-fruits of his long years of effort, aspiration and self-discipline; by no means, however, did he cease to absorb new experiences.

A new, reflective note in his verse between 1914 and 1920, was almost certainly precipitated by the First World War. This note is temporary; it is not strongly present in any of his

[1]Introduction to *My Favourite English Poems* (1950).

45

subsequent poetry, and seems to complement the war histories which he undertook at this period: such works as *Gallipoli, St. George and The Dragon, The Battle of the Somme*: these works are all remarkable for the just treatment of their subjects and the dignity of style. They are every bit as moving as books written by a poet are expected to be; they are accurate where facts are concerned; they reveal an attitude of contempt for war, of admiration for courageous action. These writings are quite free from the hysteria which infected many serious writers of the period.

In *St. George and the Dragon*, published in 1918, the poet speaks of the place and mood in which the war found him. He writes:

> In the first week of July, 1914, I was in an old house in Berkshire, a house built eight centuries before by the monks, as a place of rest and contemplation and beauty. I had never seen England so beautiful as then, and a little company of lovely friends was there. Rupert Brooke was one of them, and we read poems in that old haunt of beauty, and wandered on the Downs.

This mood is reflected in Masefield's poem *August 1914*, added to which there is the melancholy knowledge of the disaster which, in the July, was only half-sensed.

The poem *August 1914* is his first really reflective poem of note. In the slow, tempered measure reminiscent of Gray's *Elegy*, this is one of John Masefield's most successful poems. Not original in thought it none the less embodies a mood peculiarly English, which the contemplation of a still landscape evokes in times of national danger, and which, in August 1914, many must have experienced. The poet speaks of the beauty of the scene intensified by apprehension:

> How still this quiet cornfield is tonight
> By an intensest glow the evening falls
> Bringing, not darkness, but a deeper light;
> Among the stooks a partridge covey calls.

The poet next considers the unknown generations,

> Who, century after century, held these farms,
> And, looking out to watch the changing sky,
> Heard, as we hear, the rumours and alarms
> Of war at hand and danger pressing nigh.
> . . . .
> The harvest not yet won, the empty bin,
> The friendly horses taken from the stalls,
> The fallow on the hill not yet brought in,
> The cracks unplastered in the leaking walls.

Finally, comes the sort of questioning sadness, so suggestive of the spirit of those times:

> If there be any life beyond the grave,
> It must be near the men and things we love,
> . . . .
> Surely above these fields a spirit broods
> A sense of many watchers muttering near
> Of the lone Downland with the forlorn woods
> Loved to the death, inestimably dear.
>
> All the unspoken worship of those lives
> Spent in forgotten wars at other calls
> Glimmers upon these fields where evening drives
> Beauty like breath, so gently darkness falls.
>
> And silence broods like spirit on the brae,
> A glimmering moon begins, the moonlight runs
> Over the grasses of the ancient way
> Rutted this morning by the passing guns.

This is, incidentally, one of the few poems by Masefield which can stand up to close verbal analysis. Moreover, though the argument may not be acceptable to all – (in fact, on the contrary, it did strike a note of wide-felt emotion) – there *is* an argument.

Implied in the poem is the suggestion that 'life beyond the

grave' is but a shadowy, flickering reflection of terrestrial life, and that it is, in the poet's phrase, 'An influence from the Earth from those dead hearts' and 'A muttering from beyond the veils of death'.

This near-Roman concept of the soul's perpetuity in the Shades is not a surprising discovery in the 1914 ethos, nor at any time when life becomes intensified, by danger, beyond its normal proportion. But it is surprising to find this view in Masefield. He seems, on this occasion, to have given utterance to a national emotion in which his own tongue was silenced.

For here, his attitude is the complete reverse of that most natural to him. In speaking of 'the ecstatic bliss of my earliest childhood', the poet tells of thoughts and feelings which can only be described as innate Platonism. And all his writings about his early years confirm the statement that 'All that I looked upon was beautiful, and known by me to be beautiful, but also known by me to be, as it were, only the shadow of something much more beautiful. . . .'[1]

The sonnets, which appeared in 1916, seem to represent an intermittent endeavour to regain these early intimations or to win over a sceptical intellect to acceptance of them. The sonnets are attempts to find, rationally, this particular alternative to the philosophical position of the poem *August 1914*.

It is always inadvisable to try to formulate a poet's philosophy from the poems. Few poets are systematic and successful at the same time. These sonnets, which number some sixty-odd, do not conform to any logical sequence. There are a few affiliated ideas comprehensively dominating the group which may thus justifiably be called a sonnet sequence.

Beauty and Intellect, opposed always by Time and Death, form a frequent theme. Throughout, these sonnets reveal the

[1]*So Long to Learn.*

rational-humanist attitude combined with a sense of reverence for beauty. They are poems of doubt, of questioning, but not of despair. As a tribute to the sorrows, sufferings, achievements and destiny of mankind, the poems probably fulfil their purpose. In my opinion the thought is marred by the poet's exaggerated assertions of human potentialities. Such statements as those which equate 'the good God to whom none calls in vain' with 'Man's Achieved Good', which, in turn, is translated into:

> The man-made God, that man in happy breath
> Makes in despite of Time and dusty Death

offer a creed long outworn by the nineteenth century. Nor in a simply physical speculation like the following, does the poet appear to have struck any original line of thought in particular, nor any fruitful trend:

> How did the nothing come, how did these fires,
> These million-leagues of fires, first toss their hair,
> Licking the moons from heaven in their ires,
> Flinging them forth for them to wander there?
> What was the Mind? Was it a mind which thought?
> Or chance? or law? or conscious law? or power?
> Or a vast balance by vast clashes wrought?
> Or Time at trial with Matter for an hour?
> Or is it all a body where the cells
> Are living things supporting something strange,
> Whose mighty heart the singing planet swells
> As it shoulders nothing in unending change?
> Is this green earth of many-peopled pain
> Part of a life, a cell within a brain?

Again and again in these sonnets Masefield returns to the conception of 'The man-made God':

> What is the atom which contains the whole,
> This miracle which needs adjuncts so strange,
> This, which imagined God and is the soul. . . ?

which, taken a stage further, becomes,

> There is no God; but we, who breathe the air,
> Are God ourselves, and touch God everywhere.

At intervals, the theme of Platonic idealism recurs:

> Even after all these years there comes the dream
> Of lovelier life than this in some new earth
> In the full summer of that unearthly gleam.

While the sequence lacks philosophical unity, these two threads – the humanistic (roughly speaking) and the idealistic – are picked up and dropped frequently. Verbally, some of these sonnets are of great beauty and technical skill. It is noticeable that a higher quality of verse usually goes with a greater depth and maturity of thought: the one probably gives dignity to the other. Thus,

> Beauty retires; the blood out of the earth
> Shrinks, the stalk dries, lifeless November still
> Drops the brown husk of April's greenest birth.
> Through the thinned beech clump I can see the hill.
> So withers man, and though his life renews
> In Aprils of the soul, an autumn comes
> Which gives an end, not respite, to the thews
> That bore his soul through the world's martyrdoms.
> Then all the beauty will be out of mind,
> Part of man's store, that lies outside his brain,
> Touch to the dead and vision to the blind,
> Drink in the desert, bread, eternal grain,
> Part of the untilled field that beauty sows
> With flowers untold, where quickened spirit goes.

John Masefield never seemed to reconcile his conflicting theories of life, if indeed they can be called theories. He had no need to do so, for he was not a Theorist. 'Those to whom objects seem friendly,' writes Aldous Huxley, 'and who enjoy the kaleidoscopic panorama of the outside world, feel no need of an absolute.'[1] The description fits John Masefield. The external world seems friendly to him. He obviously needs no absolute. The sonnets represent a question-mark, they are inconclusive and relative; and the poet throughout implies that the meaning of life is anyone's guess. Where he does achieve consistency, however, is through the medium of his stories in prose and verse. The poet is one of those who can well demonstrate a theory but can never formulate it.

Buddhism interested John Masefield most of his life, and he certainly seemed to be temperamentally drawn to its teachings. He has written, in various dramatic forms, of the trial and crucifixion of Christ; there is very little suggestion of the Divine in these writings, but of the Enlightened – whether embodied in Christ, Gautama or some other figure – there is much.

And that, as a poet possessed of a deep sense of mystery, he found the rational-humanist position (which he propounds in various forms throughout his entire work), insufficient, is suggested by such statements as 'I believe that life is an expression of some Law or Will, that has a purpose in each of its manifestations. I believe that this world is a shadow of another world'[2] – which he has repeated in various forms elsewhere, and which is the fruition, as we have seen, of his earliest childhood faith.

VII
The Poet Laureate

John Masefield became Poet Laureate following the death in 1930 of his friend (and next-door neighbour) Robert Bridges.

[1]*Proper Studies* by Aldous Huxley (1927).
[2]*The Hereford Speech (Recent Prose* 1932 edn.).

A contemporary, Gerald Cumberland, wrote of him in 1918, 'John Masefield has an invincible picturesqueness. . . . He is tall, straight and blue-eyed, with a complexion as clear as a child's . . . you feel his sensitiveness and you admire the dignity that is at once its outcome and its protection.'[1] His appearance, in these basic particulars, changed little from that time, or indeed since the time when as a schoolgirl, I first saw him. This was shortly before or just after his appointment as Poet Laureate in 1930. I was taken to hear him read his verse in a large hall in Edinburgh.

It had been told of him that he had sailed round Cape Horn in a terrible storm, that he had experienced many adventures in South America, and that he was an awful one for swearing. We half-expected the Poet Laureate to be an immense muscular figure wearing perhaps a dark blue polo-necked sweater, sleeves rolled up to show the tattoo marks, or at least we thought he would be like those hearty and rolling merchant seamen who used to breeze up from Leith like waves of the sea themselves, at once to offend and amaze the citizens of Edinburgh. And of course the Poet Laureate turned out to be very much as described: shy, fresh-complexioned and blue-eyed. He had then that expression of perpetual surprise which he frequently wore, and which many photographs of him show.

On that occasion Masefield read parts of *Dauber* – the passage on the rounding of Cape Horn. I remember particularly how well *Minnie Maylow's Story* came over. He did not swear. His voice was remarkable. When he began to read everyone was aware that the poet was not shy, after all. He read like a true bard. Since then, I have heard many bards reading their own verse; most are diffident, some try to overcome this by over-dramatizing. I have not heard anyone read his own work like John Masefield, as if he believed in it. He read as he might have read someone else's work, and that

[1]*Set Down In Malice* (1918).

is a very difficult thing for a poet to do. His pronunciation was very pure, his tones very clear.

This impression was not illusory, for when I met Masefield about twenty years later I noticed just that unconcerned and noble quality of *speaking forth* in his ordinary conversation. So far was this from 'holding forth', that, it seemed, the quality of speech I have mentioned proceeded from the poet's natural courtesy to his listener, and not at all was it produced for *effect* (as, it must be admitted, a great deal of good speech comes forth). There is also, in Masefield's way of speaking, an element which related to the story-teller in him. He was, in this way, the type of the ancient skald. The same impulse which makes him speak with so open a voice, causes him to create his verse to be spoken aloud, and moved the poet to devote many years of his life to the cause of verse-speaking in England.

I have spoken of Masefield's look of surprise. Perhaps 'wonder' would be more accurate. There can be few men over the age of seventy who look at the world with an intense degree of wonder, as if it had just that moment been created out of chaos. In this, the expression of constant observation, I recognized again the poet I had seen as a child; then, on a platform behind a table, attended by civic functionaries and maybe an enterprising professor or two, his eyes had opened in astonishment as if at the sound of his own voice reciting *Dauber*; now, among the familiar things of his own study, he looked at them as if for the first time, with eyes more blue, if anything, by contrast with his white hair, a gleaming hard frost seen from the window behind him, and an array of blue and white china which decorated his mantelpiece.

I realized, when I met Masefield, that he did not think of himself mainly as a poet, as a novelist, a Poet Laureate, a grand old man of letters, or anything of that sort. He seemed to count it his first vocation to be a human being with an infinite curiosity about the activities of other human beings. Few living poets share with him this unselfconscious attitude. The enactment of life appears to be his first interest, both in himself and in others. As he is a writer, he defines; as he is a poet, he seeks the essential features of life; but first of all he is a participant in life. Hence, he has a genius for the seeking of phenomena themselves, and not merely what they imply. What a thing implies is in any case speculative; John Masefield starts off with experience plain.

For this, as well as for many other self-apparent reasons, I feel he was pre-eminently the poet to be Laureate. There are traditional disadvantages attached to the office; one is the traditional adulation of those who know nothing about poetry, and another is the traditional contempt of those who know something about it (Hazlitt, explaining to an audience why he refused to mourn too much the early demise of Chatterton, ex-claimed, '. . . who knows but he might have lived to be Poet Laureate?'); between these two prejudiced groups come the people who actually read the poetry written by the Laureate.

When I speak of Masefield's appropriateness for the office, I am not thinking of the short pieces he wrote for national occasions. I think these could have been better done. Other Laureates have done them better. I very much doubt if it is necessary to the spirit of Laureateship for the Laureate to write automatic odes to order. I feel this is a debased interpretation of the function of a national poet.

What I feel so decidedly qualified Masefield as Laureate, was the talent he possessed for discovering the epic element in any situation. Such works as *Gallipoli, The Nine Days' Wonder* and *Reynard the Fox* are primarily the work of a national-*minded* poet, although the first two are prose works.

Masefield, besides, worked unceasingly for the promotion of poetry. He immeasurably widened the audience for verse recitals by his encouragement of spoken verse. For a time, he had a small 'theatre' in his house at Boar's Hill. This 'room with a stage in it', as he describes it, saw many amateur productions and much experimentation amongst young poet-dramatists.

His contemporary, Herbert Palmer, told me that on a visit to Robert Bridges, then Laureate, he mentioned to his host what a fine artist John Masefield was. 'Artist!' said Robert Bridges. 'He's no artist!' It is easy to see what conscientious Bridges was driving at, when he proceeded to demonstrate certain line-by-line flaws in *Reynard the Fox*. But the composition of a successful long narrative poem needs more than the art of writing felicitous lines of verse, it needs the art of writing a long narrative poem. As an artist, Masefield was concerned with the techniques of narrative writing. And in the methods he devised of telling a story, his artistic vision is to be found.

Three

Early Poems[1]

I

It happens to be true of Masefield's poetry that his first book is the proper place to start appreciating his work. This is not the best way of approaching every poet, but with Masefield it is both convenient and necessary to begin at the beginning, since his first two collections of poems lead towards his later, more important, narrative poems.

And while I think these early pieces by no means negligible, I would not give them a place in Masefield's *opus* in proportion to the length at which I propose to discuss them. I feel it necessary to say considerably more about these poems than I would if they were to be dealt with in isolation, because of their importance in relation to the narrative poems. By this I do not mean that they are narrative poems in miniature, or that they are oblique attempts at narrative which failed. My purpose here is to try to discover the raw material of *The Everlasting Mercy*, *Reynard the Fox* and *Dauber*. For these narrative poems are not the result of a sudden brainwave; they are the natural consequence of experience already apprehended in a certain way and of the art of verse already practised in a certain way. And it is that way of apprehending and of practice which are to be sought here.

[1]The poems from *Salt Water Ballads* (1902), and *Ballads and Poems* (1910), discussed in this chapter, are available in *The Collected Poems of John Masefield* (enlarged edn. 1988, etc.).

56

II
The Created Environment of the Poems

Salt Water Ballads made an unspectacular appearance in 1902. The originality of the work was not fully recognized until *The Everlasting Mercy* made its impact nine years later. These ballads came at a time when *Barrack Room Ballads* had been popular for a decade, and John Masefield owed a lot to Kipling, in as much as he got from him confidence to use the common vernacular and a way of epitomizing a story in verse. I have already referred to the radical differences between Kipling's outlook and Masefield's and need only say here that though *Salt Water Ballads* must have seemed, on account of affinities in the use of language, to be a nautical version of *Barrack Room Ballads*, the works are near-opposite in spirit.

These early poems also appeared to be the sort of thing Sir Henry Newbolt had written and was writing about the sea. Both poets derived their forms and rhythms from sea shanties, which gave a certain similarity to their work.

What *Salt Water Ballads* offered that was fresh is to be found in the tradition it interprets – the mythology which the poet re-creates as a means of revealing his ideas. This mythology need not conform to reality but it must possess its own nature, its own consistency, harmony and discord. Now Newbolt used a ready-made mythology, comprising all the animate and otherwise Big Guns of the sea. His subjects were the British Navy, patriotism, famous Admirals, battles and glory. Kipling's mythology was akin to this, yet he made it personal to himself as a superior mind always will. He knew a lot about patriotism and glory but revealed its presence by making his characters defective in these things; he makes us see his world as from the Army ranks; he gets beneath the skin of sinners and slackers who are aware of patriotism and glory, who perform the duties entailed because they have no other choice, but who have no natural inclination to play up and play Sir Henry Newbolt's game.

Masefield's world resembles Kipling's only so far as he, too, is concerned with the 'ranks'. His men, however, are a more heterogeneous lot, merchant servicemen who have signed on for service in the last of the sailing ships in every port of the globe. Danes, Cockneys, Asiatics, South Americans – the sort of mixed bunch to be found in Conrad's *Nigger of the Narcissus*. Their wellbeing is not, so far as we are made aware, ensured by the knowledge that in the last resort there will always be the presence of a British, or any other, Consul to demand. When they sign on they relinquish national claims and protection and adopt the new loyalties and communal rights of sailing ships. It is not only that allegiance is transferred temporarily from civic authority to ship's captain. The captain, in this world which Masefield shows us, is usually no more than a silhouette, an order, a shout, an inconstant element to be taken for granted like the sea itself. Kipling would have made these captains *felt* in his world had he treated more aspects of the sea than he did, in any detail. The captain and officers would have been to the men much like a Commissioner of Police and his force on land. Not so in the world of *Salt Water Ballads*, where the cosmology or set-up is centred within the Ship. The Ship, the way she is handled, her peculiarities, her tyrannies, the marvels she can perform, her cargo, her fate – it is the Ship that embraces the crew, the officers and the captain. She exacts penalties and allegiances, dispenses protection and favours; her boundaries are those of the whole of the world of *Salt Water Ballads*.

And that world is not entirely indicated by the much-quoted but misleading *A Consecration* with which *Salt Water Ballads* begins:

Not of the princes and prelates with periwigged
    charioteers
Riding triumphantly laurelled to lap the fat of the
    years –
Rather the scorned – the rejected – the men hemmed in
    with the spears;

which is often referred to as the sort of first principle of
Masefield's work – understandably, because he ends with
the line:

Of these shall my songs be fashioned, my tales be told.
                                        Amen.

which I regard merely as the gesture of a young poet
passionately dedicated to humanity. With *Reynard the Fox* he
quite clearly shifted his position, not to remove himself from
the human cause but to observe it more entirely. His work is
by no means so one-sided as this early poem suggested it
would turn out to be, nor even was his first book. The world
of *Salt Water Ballads* is better located if we concentrate on the
epigraph to the book, for a writer who knows what he is
about does not quote a passage at the beginning of his work
as an adornment only, but because it is a kind of clue, and
such a clue is present in the lines:

The mariners are a pleasant people, but little like those in the
towns, and they can speak no other language than that used in
ships.

(*The Licenciate Vidriera.*)

This gently suggestive passage has a precise bearing on the
poems to follow and a general connection with all Masefield's writings about the sea. Here the poetic justification for
exploring the subject is revealed, that is, the discovery by the
poet of a world of which the ship is the perimeter enclosing
men who gauge their conduct by, and use the language of,
ships. It is not the picturesque way of looking at things, for

that would be to give the mariners' world a self-conscious harmony which is not present in *Salt Water Ballads*.

The way in which Masefield sees this world is a detached one, although it is familiar to him. He extracts a kind of beauty from the words, the actions, the characteristics of sailors, which are of no beauty whatsoever to the sailors; had he not been a sailor he would not know this world he describes, and were he not detached he would not find beauty in it. Hence the paradox that while the poet identifies himself with the observer, he identifies himself also with the observed; and the paradox is reconciled in the fact that the poet is aware both of the spirit of the sea-faring world, and the formal expression of it – its ritual and dogma, one might say. The one interprets the other.

As to the spirit: Masefield is well-versed, accurate and sensitive to every detail. Most important, he is always specific. You never find him writing about the sea in general or about seamen in general. To interpret the spirit of anything, it requires not to be vague.

As to the 'ritualistic' side of the seaman's world, this is conveyed by formulae which consist of a certain language and certain characteristics to which generations of multi-national merchant seamen have contributed. Popular cults, religions, superstitious beliefs, dialects and attitudes have been thrown together, have stuck together, have merged, have erased each other or have survived, and are now seen as a conglomerate culture, somewhat unevenly distributed.

The world of *Salt Water Ballads* is entirely concrete. Note the glossary of sea terms provided by the poet. They are concrete, technical, specialized and, at times, so apt as to be almost self-descriptive. The glossary is as much a part of the poems as the epigraph. The explanations of terms are worded with care. The glossary is a binding agent to the poems (though I doubt if the conscious intention of the poet – who often provides glossaries and maps with his work – was other than thoughtfulness for the reader). To quote from the fascinating list:

Abaft the Beam — That half of a ship included between her amid-ship section and the taffrail.

Advance note — A note for one month's wages issued to sailors on their signing a ship's articles.

Bloody — An intensive derived from the substantive 'blood', a name applied to the Bucks, Scowrers, and Mohocks of the seventeenth and eighteenth centuries.

Bonded Jacky — Negro-head tobacco or sweet cake.

Bull of Barney — A beast mentioned in an unquotable sea-proverb.

Cape Horn Fever — The illness proper to malingerers.

Chanty — A song sung to lighten labour at the capstan, sheets, and halliards. The soloist is known as the chantyman, and is usually a person of some authority in the fo'c's'le. Many chanties are of great beauty and extreme antiquity.

Fore-Stay — A powerful wire rope supporting the foremast forward.

Gaskets — Ropes or plaited lines used to secure the sails in furling.

Goneys — Albatrosses.

Port Mahon Baboon, or *Port Mahon Soger* — I have been unable to discover either the origin of these insulting epithets or the reasons for the peculiar bitterness with which they sting the marine recipient. They are older than Dana (*circa* 1840).

An old merchant sailor, now dead, once told me that Port Mahon was that godless city from which the Ark set sail, in which case the name may have some traditional connection with that evil 'Mahoun' or 'Mahu', prince of darkness, mentioned by Shakespeare and some of our older poets.

The real Port Mahon, a fine harbour in Minorca, was taken by the French, from Admiral Byng, in the year 1756.

I think that the phrases originated at the time of Byng's consequent trial and execution.

Soger — A laggard, malingerer, or hang-back. To loaf or skulk or work Tom Cox's Traverse.

Spunyarn — A three-strand line spun out of old rope-yarns knotted together. Most sailing-ships carry a spunyarn

> winch, and the spinning of such yarn is a favourite
> occupation in fine weather.
>
> *Tackle* — Pronounced 'taykle'. A combination of pulleys for
> obtaining of artificial power.

These words have a practical purpose beyond their immediate one of definition, for they make us consider seriously the world of the poems, and discourage that condescension towards a supposed quaint charm with which people are prone to view a small community outside their own experience. It is true that the item 'Bloody — An intensive derived from the substantive "blood" . . .' is presented tongue-in-cheek, but on the whole the glossary helps to make pretty plain that the ballads are not fresh-water.

Most of these ballads take the form of stories told by the seamen – a form that is dropped in Masefield's next book, *Ballads and Songs* (1903; reprinted in 1910 as *Ballads and Poems*), which however should be read in conjunction with *Salt Water Ballads*. The form is a useful one for introducing the characteristics of the community, the first being of course their extreme garrulity – their defence against boredom.

It seems to be true of any unmixed or specialist community whose members are forced to live together at close quarters, that by unacknowledged, instinctive and common consent, certain events – which may seem quite trivial – take on the features of myth, the dimensions of which increase with time and frequent communication.

Thus, the type of communal mythology which Masefield shows us is part of the sailor's life (it is present among school-children, soldiers and even families – any enclosed and identifiable social unit, in fact) – this type of mythology is akin to tradition, but tradition is more conscious, more organized, than is this elementary and primitive instinct to 'legendarize' isolated events, and so bind together imaginatively a community already closely bound by material necessity. Tradition, moreover, is nearer to the concept of

Convention (which is redeemed by becoming Law before it degenerates into Red Tape), than it is to its source in the mythological system of a social group.

The *tradition* of the sailors' existence is apparent in *Salt Water Ballads* (we will find evidence of convention, law and red tape too); but where Masefield is unique is in capturing this deeper, older, more elusive phenomenon, their mythology.

As 'solemn gospel' the men pass on to each other bits of practical advice, tips about health, magnified tales of past adventures, scraps of folklore which testify both to their discrepant origins and to their common existence.

> 'I sets no store upon stooards – they ain't no use on
> a ship.'
> > (*Sing a Song O' Shipwreck*).

declares one man.

> 'And I give you a gospel truth when I state
> The crowd didn't find any fault with the Mate,'
> > (*The Yarn of The Loch Achray*).

says another. These are the voices of tradition: mates are unpopular and stewards useless. There is also convention: the principal convention recognized by these men is a basic callousness on which are superimposed all sorts and shades of personal sentiment, as in *Burial Party*, the last verse of which is an example of seafaring mythology – the original event lost forever, yet forever perpetuated, perpetually enlarged, in the telling.

> ' 'N' all the night till the grey o' the dawn the dead
> 'un has to swim
> With a blue 'n' beastly Will o' the Wisp a-burnin'
> over him,
> With a herring, maybe, a-scoffin' a toe or a shark
> a-chewin' a limb.'

There is a good deal of miscellaneous speculation as to what happens to a mariner's spirit after death. Here again, the seafaring community feels a wish to preserve its identity from that of the landsmen. The soul of a mariner has a fate all its own, however miscellaneous the details. *Sea-Change* contributes such a legend:

> 'Goneys an' gullies an' all o' the birds o' the sea
>   They ain't no birds, not really,' said Billy the Dane.
> 'Not mollies, nor gullies, nor goneys at all,' said he,
>   'But simply the sperrits of mariners livin' again.'

and *Cape Horn Gospel I* another:

> " 'I'm a-weary of them there mermaids,'
> Says old Bill's ghost to me;
> 'It ain't no place for a Christian
> Below there – under sea.
> For it's all blown sand and shipwrecks,
> And old bones eaten bare,
> And them cold fishy females
> With long green weeds for hair.

Nostalgia is always present in this mental environment. The nostalgia itself is an essential part of the world of sailing ships in their decline. The encroachment of the steam vessel gives the emotion an impetus: 'Hear that P. and O. boat's engines dronin'' (*A Ballad of Cape St. Vincent*). But where he demonstrates nostalgia, Masefield is apt to lose sight of his object, and is drawn into the then fashionable nostalgic modes of Yeats and his followers of that time. For the purpose of what Masefield was doing at this time, for what he was writing in a new way, Yeats was not the best influence.

It is very often difficult for a poet to convey in an original manner an emotion which has become the supreme motif of a greater poet dominating his own age. Yeats had been very successfully nostalgic at the time of *Salt Water Ballads*, and so where a nostalgia indigenous to sailing ships was required in John Masefield's collection, we have the 'Aedh wishes for' sigh of the Celtic Twilight, present but out of place:

> A wind's in the heart of me, a fire's in my heels,
> I am tired of brick and stone and rumbling wagon-
>   wheels;

The results are often quite successful, seen as exercises in the mode of the 'nineties. But this Yeatsian tinge, where it occurs, detracts from the integrity of the sea poems; the nostalgia proper to the poem is lost. This factor is really connected with the language of *Salt Water Ballads* and *Ballads and Poems*, which will be examined presently so far as the styles of the 'nineties, of Yeats and of Rossetti seem to be imposed upon the basic idiom which John Masefield is at this stage attempting to utilize. The point to be observed at present is that, where the imaginative environment of the work is concerned, the introduction of a 'literary' quality to nostalgia makes the emotion seem spurious, obtrusive, not part of the whole.

It was not until later in his life that Masefield came to handle successfully this element of nostalgia. Whether the sailors experience a longing for the sea (when on land) as in *Sea-Fever*, or for the land (when at sea) as in *The West Wind*, or whether the nostalgia is localized – focused on a few square yards of English soil as in *Hell's Pavement*; whether the sailor is yearning for some tropical sea or island as in *Spanish Waters*, or whether it represents the general mood induced by the decline of sailing ships, nostalgia dominates the sea life that Masefield sets out to portray.

Two further elements contribute to the scene these poems present us with: aspects of roughness, sickness, danger, crudity and horror in contrast with visual richness. Both extremes of sea life are communicated with that whole realism which, in land life, admits the rose-tree as well as the slag-heap, and of which Masefield has made particular use throughout his work. *Port of Holy Peter* (from *Ballads and Poems*) gives the atmosphere of specific horror at the same time as the theme is generalized (partly through the impersonal ballad lilt employed). We are caused to believe that the Port is both a unique place (as it is 'identified' by detailed description) and a typical one (since it is 'Spanish port', 'Fever port', and because the things that go on there include 'stabbing, of course,'). In this exceptional poem – one of John Masefield's best – the vividness of the picture evoked and the vividness of the horror combine, are telescoped.

But the more intimate horror – the every-day discomforts of life on board ship, are what we are mostly made aware of; 'chewing salted horse and biting flinty bread'. And the horror (conveyed though it is in the form of a tall story) comes through as something altogether real in such grim humour as the following (note the irony of the fourth line, suggestive of a mixed body of beliefs):

> Josey slipped from the tops'l-yard an' bust his bloody
> back
> (Which comed from playing the giddy goat an' leavin'
> go the jack);
> We lashed his chips in clouds of sail an' ballasted him
> with stones,
> 'The Lord hath taken away,' we says, 'an' we give him
> to Davy Jones.'
> An' that was afore we were up with the Line.
> (*Cape Horn Gospel II.*)

Those other realities – the wealth and diversity of foreign ports, the profusion of colour, as in *Harbour-Bar*, and of sound, as in *St. Mary's Bells*, the perpetual sensuous variety, as in *Trade Winds*, and the variety of changing sea and sky, of *Cardigan Bay* – these balance the monotony and horror of the life portrayed in *Salt Water Ballads*.

The ship itself synthesizes the whole scene; the ship is always shown to be the worth-while thing, her parts are named with respect, and skill in handling her is reckoned higher than any abstract principles (of which these men give utterance to very few). It is the ship which carries the cargo, baffles the elements or else is baffled, and which bears the men to distant countries.

To the sailors, the ship is what the earth is to the agricultural landsman. It is not merely a means of earning a living or fulfilling a vocation. The ship does not signify for the sailors simply what it does for the owners – a means of carrying cargo; in fact cargoes are not often mentioned in these poems, except to make a fanciful juxtaposition of the old with the new, as in the well-known poem *Cargoes*. For the sailors, the ship, while they are aboard, is life, and every job to be done is part of life:

> Spunyarn, spunyarn, with one to turn the crank,
> And one to slather the spunyarn, and one to knot the
>   hank;

'Life is nothing but spunyarn', the poet continues.

From this point Masefield's later writings about the sea do not diverge; and one of the most important things about this early work is that it outlines the system within which the narrative poem *Dauber* or, for instance, the novel *Bird of Dawning*, can be identified.

III
Language

Not all the poems included with *Salt Water Ballads* are part of the scheme or world examined above. These other poems are mainly lyrics in the current style of Yeats, but drawing more distantly on the 'nineties of Arthur Symons, Ernest Dowson and Laurence Binyon, and, farther back, from Swinburne and Rossetti.

The difference between *Salt Water Ballads* and *Ballads and Poems* can best be appreciated from the language. In the latter book, the poet is more consciously the poet, he seems to stand more outside his subject. Many of the poems which appear in this volume are successful as minor pieces of the period, but they do not bear that signature, that personal stamp which is a feature of his first book. What these poems show most clearly is the kind of idiom Masefield was at the time overcoming, as if trying to speak through a hum of other voices which, none the less, he felt the need to listen to.

Sorrow of Mydath (from *Salt Water Ballads*) may be taken as an example of this complication of nostalgic decadence with a phraseology not entirely Masefield's own. Its second line, 'Weary the heart and the mind and the body of me', is not Masefield's voice, nor is the feeling expressed convincing, the latter being probably a result of the former.

The desire for annihilation, so compulsive in late Romantic poetry, is outside Masefield's orbit; and it is possible that at this period he found it difficult, as young poets often do, to resist using a way of speech he found attractive in older poets, and more difficult still to avoid affecting the attitudes which went with the idiom. We find, therefore, inconsistencies within the poem which derive from a lack of sincerity in the vision.

The image, in the second stanza, of an 'outcast, derelict soul' is obviously blurred: sympathy is invited for the outcast because he is 'drenched with the spindrift', and it is again invited because he is 'athirst' not for fresh water but apparently for more salt. It is true that 'the cool green waves of death' are partly figurative while the spindrift is actual, but here the actual and the figurative are not so different as to justify their use in contradictory statements. Again we find that the waves are required to 'arise and burst/In a tide of quiet', which is difficult to imagine happening.

The poem is the sort of thing the best poets of the 'nineties wrote, but only the sort of thing. Not an attitude, but the shadow of an attitude, and sometimes the shadow of a shadow, are revealed. There is not only the nostalgia of early Yeats present in the lines:

A wind's in the heart of me, a fire's in my heels,
I am tired of brick and stone and rumbling wagon-
      wheels;

> I hunger for the sea's edge, the limits of the land,
> Where the wild old Atlantic is shouting on the sand.
>   (*A Wanderer's Song.*)

but also of the French Symbolists strained through Arthur Symons. Note Symons' similar theme in his poem, also entitled *Wanderer's Song* (1898):

> I have had enough of women and enough of love,
> But the land waits, and the sea waits and day and night
>   is enough;
> Give me a long white road, and the grey white path
>   of the sea,
> And the wind's will and the bird's will, and the heart-
>   ache still in me.

John Masefield's poem certainly arises from a more sincere and lasting emotion than does Arthur Symons'. This fact, however, is not revealed by the text of the poems but by what we know of the personalities of the respective authors. As a poem, Symons' is more convincing. He got the real thing from the French, but even then his own affectation adds something. By the time the theme reaches Masefield it has lost all individual character, and is merely a restatement.

But both poets, in the instances quoted above, are tangled in a lattice-work of echoes, and echoes of echoes. Consequently, 'day and night is enough', writes Arthur Symons, for the purpose merely of lengthening the line in some impressionistic way; and Masefield slipping all unawares into the sentiment of being 'tired of' something, hits on 'wagon-wheels' – which has every appearance of being no more than a convenient rhyme with 'heels'. Swinburne was far more direct and effective when he wrote:

> I will go back to the great sweet mother,
> Mother and lover of men, the sea.

and so is Masefield in his celebrated *Sea-Fever*, where there is no question of the desire for the sea being precipitated by a dislike of the land. It is not really in Masefield's nature as a poet to be tired of anything, as he soon, it would seem, discovered.

But in his early work, we hear from time to time these derivative echoes, with the poet's own voice coming through in varying proportions, until at last he found his own tongue. Occasionally, these poems in someone else's manner possess qualities which compensate for lack of originality – those compact formal qualities which lead us to say a poem is well written, but which lead us no further.

There is an element of mimicry in all good poets, discernible generally in their early work; and this is only to repeat what many others have said, that the influences of other poets have to be properly assimilated. Till then, a poet is a slave, and he has to 'squeeze the slave out of himself' where poetry is concerned, as Chekhov notoriously re-marked where life was concerned.

I stress the point that the freedom necessary to a poet is a matter of language. It does not matter how original his thought, how profound his knowledge, how new his themes, he will not be a free poet nor be able to offer original thought until he discovers his personal way of putting things.

The interesting early experiment with impressionist form expressed in Masefield's poem *On Eastnor Knoll* falls into banality simply because the language is not altogether the poet's own:

> A bright white star blinks, the pale moon rounds, but
> Still the red, lurid wreckage of the sunset
> Smoulders in smoky fire, and burns on
> The misty hill-tops.
>
> Ghostly it grows, and darker, the burning
> Fades into smoke, and now the gusty oaks are
> A silent army of phantoms thronging
> A land of shadows.

But note 'lurid wreckage of the sunset' and 'the gusty oaks': the poet's authentic voice finding its way through the time-dishonoured 'silent army of phantoms thronging / A land of shadows.'

What we often find in these first poems is the circumstance common to young poets, of the poem being submerged by poetry, the specific conception to be expressed being submerged by the aggregate conception already expressed by others. That is why John Masefield is most successful, at this stage, when he is dealing with situations unknown to the recent poetry of his time, as in the real salt-water pieces where his own resources are called into play, and his own style uninhibited. His own style is the result, as generally is the case, of experiment. With the epigraph to *Salt Water Ballads* in mind, which tells us that the mariners 'can speak no other language than that used in ships;' we can see how Masefield experimented with fitting the common idiom of the sailing ship world to the needs of verse. He had to use some of the equipment of poetry which would not normally be used in the speech he wanted to reproduce; and, more difficult, he had to use the idiomatic equipment which had not yet appeared in poetry. And very often the necessary fusion is accomplished by the use of a single word:

> When the rising moon was a copper disc and the sea
> was a strip of steel,
> We dumped him down to the swaying weeds ten
> fathom beneath the keel.
>
> (*Bill.*)

'Dumped' is the word which keeps the lines free to say what the poet wants them to say – that a dead sailor was being disposed of from a sailing ship. They would naturally dump him down, and naturally speak of having dumped him. Change the word to 'lowered' or 'set' and the lines become a piece of late nineteenth-century verse of vague origin. It is true that the sailors would not naturally speak of the rising moon as 'a copper disc' nor of the sea 'as a strip of steel', but it does not matter because in a poem the effect is the thing, and we are constantly made aware of the effect of common speech. Common speech as it is spoken, word for word, would of course be intolerable in any form of writing. The technique which John Masefield now began to use in his narrative verse is that of juxtaposing two forms of rhetorical speech – that which has become high and hallowed by poetic usage, and that which represents – not merely reproduces – common vernacular. It is a technique we are used to finding in modern poetry, but we should not forget that Masefield was a pioneer exponent of it in the present century.

At the beginning of this century Masefield was capable of writing in a derivative, late-Romantic manner; not merely competently but with positive success which he could have developed to the mould of his own talent. *The Dead Knight* shows he could present a universal theme in a personal way. This poem, where diction is concerned, is one of the 'tightest' in the collection; it points to a path Masefield might have taken but did not take. If he had exploited his talent for gentle, ironical lament, it would have possibly been the easier course, he would possibly have developed as a better craftsman, and within a few years he would have occupied a leading place in the short-lived Georgian regime.

But he had other kinds of experiences to express, which needed a much looser colloquial idiom:

> You can take 'n' tell Nan I'm goin' about the world
> agen,
> 'N' that the world's wide.
> > (*A Valediction (Liverpool Docks)*.)

and,

> Loafin' around in Sailor Town, a-bluin' o' my advance,
> > (*One of the Bo'sun's Yarns.*)

The 'looseness', however, is in the phraseology, relaxed to

suit the rhythms of the sailors' conversation. The diction itself is not slack in the sense of being careless; it is easy speech, but not easy to make a poem from. The lines are constantly being made taut by the use of arresting and vivid verbs, sometimes belonging to the language of ships and sometimes coined by the poet (the italics are mine):

Where the sunlight *shudders* golden round about.

. . . . . .

'I shall hear them *hilly-hollying* the weather crojick
    brace,'

                            (*The Turn of the Tide.*)

The fact that the most importantly-used words are verbs (a point to be noted in all Masefield's work) may have some significance: since the Elizabethan dramatists the verb as a dynamic in relation to poetic context has been on the decline. It is simply that the poetry of action tends to rely upon the verb, while the poetry of ideas and description puts the weight of meaning on other parts of speech.

Masefield's poetry is seldom sedentary, and never so when at its best. We must look for action in his most typical, most enduring work. Nevertheless, he is no dramatist, so it does not hold that wherever he deals with action he is successful.

Action and dialogue in the poems very often, in fact, replace imagery, and this is particularly true of the narrative poems. John Masefield's use of metaphor and simile to evoke an image is not sparing, but rarely vivid. But his work is vivid on a large scale, depending upon an accumulation of rhythm, action, dialogue and plain description.

IV

Experiments with Form

The main difference between *Salt Water Ballads* and the second collection *Ballads and Poems* is the attempt in the latter to tighten up slack phraseology which the earlier colloquial ease had demanded. The poet was led to explore the possibilities of new forms and rhythms adaptable to new themes. He had already explored the potentialities of the sea chanty as a basis for the *Salt Water* pieces, and had effected a range of variations on the sea chanty with successful mastery. In this second book the poet does not attempt to exploit the *Salt Water* genre. He imposes upon himself the discipline required by the technical problems in the form-theme region.

I intend a distinction, which I ought to explain here, when I speak of the new forms with which the poet experiments, and his search for suitable form for his themes. My excuse for this digression is that form applied to poetry is a particularly nebulous term, yet a necessary one. We speak of poetry for instance as an art-form. We say of verse which appears in a regular metrical pattern that it is formal: irregular verse is frequently called informal. Yet we can say of a poem that it takes the form of free verse; that another poem (however shapeless) takes the form of a narrative; and that another poem is in the sonnet-form.

It is clear, then, that when we speak of what pertains to 'form' in different contexts, we speak of different things. The confusion arises where we are forced to use the same word to convey different things in the same context. Then, to confound the confusion, we are bound to recognize the overlapping of meanings: 'form' in one context is not entirely dissimilar from 'form' in another. And when we remember that the application of the idea 'form' to poetry is borrowed from other arts, and is used in connection with activities outside art, the concept of order which we denote as 'form' becomes well-nigh chaotic (so ironically does enthusiastic usage return upon itself).

When I refer to the forms employed by the poet, I mean the structural arrangement of his verse: a technical matter which includes the metre and length of the lines, the number of lines to each verse, the order of words in so far as this is structurally determined; the quality of the terms: I mean the devices[1] of his verse.

When, however, I suggest that the poet experiments with these technical methods of verse in order to arrive at the appropriate 'form' for his theme, and that this activity is leading him towards a narrative 'form', I mean there the order and degree in which his ideas are presented. This definition is meant to embrace the qualities of selection and rejection which the poet must practise in recreating his experience. What is left unsaid in a poem is perhaps as important as what is said. It is the instinct for selection of experience as well as of words which tells the poet at what point he will start revealing his conception of the whole and at what point he will conclude. Between these two points there will be various degrees and intensities of revelation. And he will not reveal the whole conception by telling the whole story word by word; the pattern or shape of what he chooses to reveal will act as his mouthpiece.

Ultimately, it is this poetic-form (the second definition) rather than the verse-form which helps us to recognize the work of a particular poet as distinct from all others. But the two types of 'form' are correlated, in so far as the pattern of words and the pattern of poetic thought (not the thought itself) are technical matters, depending one on the other. A danger for the poet, and especially the beginner, seems always to present itself when the verse-form or pattern of words he employs (usually in a derivative manner) dominates the poetic-form or pattern of thought. It is a danger present in any fixed species of poetry, like the sonnet where the pattern of words so frequently imposes the 'sonnet'

[1] These 'devices, . . . peculiar to the poetic language', distinguished by John Crowe Ransom as 'Spreaders', 'Rufflers', 'Importers' and 'Meters' seem to me the most economic definition of verse forms I have seen. They are introduced and explained in his *Towards an Understanding of Poets* (*Wordsworth* ed. Gilbert Dunklin P & P. 1951).

sentiment. So that, in attempting to find a poetic-form suitable to a theme, the poet must always be occupied with obtaining equity through the verse-forms he employs.

I come back to Masefield, to show that at the *Ballads and Poems* stage he was not so much intent on stating new themes (he had already done so) as preparing for narrative verse in many themes. This preparation I believe he went about instinctively in the right way – by exercising the technical aspects of verse in their relation to a given theme.

The interesting poem *An Old Song Re-Sung* belongs to this collection and has something of the exercise-piece about it. *The Gentle Lady* is an exercise in pure lyricism; that is, with attention mainly given to the first needs of the lyric – a melodious and rhythmic arrangement of words – without much regard to a literal meaning; the 'meaning' itself being no more than a key-note.

To some of these forms, though he managed them well, the poet does not often return in his later work: almost unique in his opus, for example, is *The Wild Duck*, an impressionistic poem with a strong atmosphere. But in other cases, Masefield began to employ forms particularly suited to themes he develops later. His sensitivity to the great associations of history, has its first appearance here. And because any theme which involves an imaginative response to history is in danger of becoming diffuse, Masefield places such themes in a compact form.

In this, *Malvern Hill* (from *Salt Water Ballads*) may be compared with *Fragments* and *The Harper's Song* (from *Ballads and Poems*). It is not that the last two poems are superior as poems to *Malvern Hill*, which is one of Masefield's best in this genre, but that he was attempting more difficult things at the expense of originality and was moving in his own right direction. For this reason, the *Poems* in *Ballads and Poems* seem to me more important than the *Ballads*, since in the former the poet was practising, if he did not master, a new lyrical compactness in a variety of rhythms; and without a basic lyricism, without rhythmic variety and above all, without compactness, a long narrative poem of the kind presently to be written would be merely long-winded.

To make a very wide generalization, then, I would say that in Masefield's first collection we have the poet speaking from the inside, and occupied principally with the poetry of each poem; while in his second collection he is the poet from the outside occupied mainly with verse. Many have taken the opposite view. The following, for instance, in *Salt Water Ballads*,

> Her crew were shipped and they said 'Farewell,
> So-long, my Tottie, my lovely gell;
> We sail to-day if we fetch to hell,
> It's time we tackled the wheel a spell.'
> (*The Yarn of The Loch Achray.*)

is from a certain viewpoint, verse (i.e. the form without the spirit).

> So beautiful, so dainty-sweet,
> So like a lyre's delightful touch –
> A beauty perfect, ripe, complete
> That art's own hand could only smutch
> And nature's self not better much.
> (*The Gentle Lady.*)

in *Ballads and Poems* is, from that same viewpoint, which I believe to be wrong, poetry.

And I hope to have shown, from my opposite view, that the originality and intensity of vision in *Salt Water Ballads* was something which had to be expressed at this stage of the poet's career; that, at the second stage, his necessity was for practising the craft of poetry; and the second collection, though as poetry it is unoriginal and derivative, was important to his art since it gave the necessary practice. For John Masefield did not practise verse-forms with a view to practising more verse, but to practising poetry.

V

We come back to the beginning: both collections, taken together, lead to the narrative poems, and that, for the purpose of a study of Masefield's work, is of great significance. Though the world of the sea which makes the background of *Salt Water Ballads* is not in direct evidence in the first of his narrative poems, it is to return in *Dauber* (and is already present in the prose writings). But the ability to create a physical environment, a setting – the employment of this technique in new circumstances, rather than the repetition of one manifestation of it, is what we should look for. This is already successfully apparent in *The Everlasting Mercy*.

And at a later stage, the poet's aptitude for creating a whole 'world' as a setting for his work reaches out from one work to another: for example, the exceptionally interesting system of landscape, towns, villages, pubs and people which links *Reynard the Fox* with the novels and with other poems.

Then we have seen his experiments with language, both to express as from inside a particular social group, its colloquial essence, and to express from outside a particular situation, the poetic comment on that situation. These very qualities were later to animate the narrative poems. Different environments requiring a different idiom, different situations requiring different comments, were to be shown in the narrative poems, but the skill had already been acquired.

So, too, his experiments both with verse-forms and with forms of expression created in the poet the verbal flexibility, the adaptability to changing situations, which are essential to narrative poetry.

The points I have summarized here are technical ones. There is, of course, more to the making of a poem like *Reynard the Fox* than technique. The vision was there to begin with; and I attach first importance to the technical aspects of poetry because they are the agents for the 'given' factors of illumination and elucidation; it is only a successful poetic technique which confirms the vision as a poetic one.

The vision was there to start with; it is but fragmentarily revealed through the early poems. In *Salt Water Ballads* there is a poem which I feel is important from its being more in the nature of a prophetic assertion than most of the others; it is a statement which contains a glimpse of what John Masefield's poetic vision was, and how it was to develop:

> Faces – passionate faces – of men I may not know,
> They haunt me, burn me to the heart, as I turn aside
>   to go.
> The king's face and the cur's face, and the face of the
>   stuffed swine,
> They are passing, they are passing, their eyes look
>   into mine.
>
> ('*All Ye That Pass By.*')

Four

The Narrative Poems:
An Introductory Note

'Also, of course, they can be read as stories' – so the late Charles Williams ends an essay on Victorian narrative poetry.[1] The theme of the essay is, appropriately, the moral content of Victorian narrative verse which is based (as Williams, from a religious standpoint, saw it) on a concept of conduct which is both a means and an end – conduct without a supernatural significance to it, only a social one. I think this is an appropriate way to start sizing up Victorian narrative verse, because it happens that Browning and Tennyson and Matthew Arnold were writing about conduct. The story was primarily used as a demonstration of the ethic; the story was a substitute for behaviour, and only when that greater intensity of behaviour which really deserves the name of action ran away with the poet, did the story seem to have its own being. Therefore, to read these poems as stories is to make an alternative reading. '*Also*, of course, they can be read as stories.'

Masefield started where the Victorians left off; not quite so abruptly as that, of course, for though he, like Kipling and Chesterton, was writing verse in the reign of Queen Victoria, he consummated a belated tendency to return to the original business of narrative verse which is to tell a story. Masefield wrote to me: 'My main concern has always

[1] *A Book of Victorian Narrative Verse*. Chosen By Charles Williams (1927).

80

been to tell stories, and to learn how to do this with effect by word of mouth to living audiences; trying verse, because I loved verse, and know its power upon hearers; trying prose, because the design sometimes imposed it.'[1] So, I begin where Charles Williams left off. Masefield's narrative poems must first be read as poetry; you can extract the philosophical essence, the ethical tone can be got at, you can assess the verse, the technical structure; but you must read them first as stories and judge every other quality with constant reference to the requirements of the story.

When Masefield says that his main concern has always been to tell stories 'and to learn how to do this with effect to living audiences' he says two things which ought to be borne in mind on coming to the narrative poems, the central body of his work. First, the poems were made to be spoken, and so, if possible, they should be read aloud. At least they should be read with an attentive ear. Secondly, we should know that the 'living audiences' included more than poetry-reading, poetry-loving people. Masefield's art is not a high-brow art, though that does not exclude intellectual appreciation. However, it was not written for intellectuals but for people (not 'the people' far less the mob, but the people who are likely to listen to a story). I should also explain that when I say it is not written for intellectuals I am trying to define Masefield's art, not to evaluate it: the practice of using the word 'intellectual' as a term of abuse, or on the other hand the word 'popular' as a term of contempt, is common but is as ineffectual for critical purposes as it is for the purposes of abuse and contempt.

The number of people who are likely to listen to a story still amounts to a lot of people, although they are fewer today than in 1911. Cinema and television are the most popular story-telling agencies at present, where the spoken word is a mere commentary on the visual effects – the dialogue is

[1]Letter to the Author May 24, 1951.

simply the caption of silent films in a more developed manifestation; and in its pure form the film is a silent art. For the language of the cinema at its best is not dramatic, in the sense that the language of the theatre at its best is dramatic. Film-speech confirms, defines, emphasizes the action, dramatic speech dominates the action to the point of transfiguring it. Story-telling at present when addressed to most 'living audiences' is therefore done by visual means. But there still remains a vast living audience that listens to stories. Before going any further I should say why I am bypassing the comparatively large novel-reading public; this is because I see novel-reading as a private affair; the novel is threatened as well as the narrative poem, though to a lesser extent, by the film; the novel has never (until the recent welcome broadcasting experiences) been listened to by an audience. When I say that there still exist vast audiences who listen to stories, I am thinking of those many thousands (many thousands more than listen to broadcast novels) who listen to broadcast commentaries on national events – cup-ties, the Derby, State processions. It is possible, therefore, that radio and television commentators are the present-day counterpart of the ancient bard who got up and gave utterance. To be a public commentator is now the vocation for the born narrator. If we want to know something of the excitement transmitted by the spoken story in the past, we will find it in the excitement these commentators send over the air: the commentary on the Grand National is a story – the modern form of epic which owes its form (eye-witness) to a widespread belief in actual events and a corresponding disbelief in events imaginatively presented, however historically accurate.[1] I think this indicates a deep desire in all people for a spoken story. The need to hear a story cannot, I think, be satisfied by the seeing of it.

It should be noted how at times Masefield anticipates the

[1] Coleridge's 'willing suspension of disbelief' has ceased to evoke *willingness*.

modern commentator – see the close of the race in *Right Royal*, the account of the fight in *The Everlasting Mercy*, the last lap of the fox's flight in *Reynard the Fox*.

These poems could not have been written without a conception of a 'living audience' being present to the poet. We should be aware of this fact when we read them; indeed, we are made aware of it by the poems themselves – their directness, the uncomplicated and vigorous emotions they depict. It is not that they aim at a low common average of understanding, but that they get at those fundamental responses which are commonly shared. In this they differ from any narrative verse before Tam O'Shanter: even Crabbe confines his scope (and, of course, attracts our curiosity) by dealing with subtle, complex, aberrational feelings. Browning, Tennyson, large as their audiences were, addressed nothing like the variety of people Masefield began to write for in 1911. Browning and Tennyson wrote for the literate middle-class who wanted to read poetry; these poets' moral preoccupations showed all the subtlety of compromise which could reach as far as, and beyond, the understanding of society's most powerful members. Masefield, addressing a public of all classes who still retained a certain naïvety along with their new literacy, had the task of touching chords which were at once elementary and universal.

I have already spoken of the 'purity' of motive which associates Masefield as a narrative poet with Chaucer. There is a vast difference between Chaucer's audience and Masefield's but not so vast a difference as between Chaucer's audience and Tennyson's. Chaucer addresses a literate and comparatively unsophisticated audience; so, in spite of other differences, does Masefield. Tennyson's audience was a much more complex affair. We should be aware, when reading Masefield's narratives, of this quality in the audience he speaks to, for it is a type of audience which has since disappeared. For this reason alone, we shall probably admire in his works elements other than those which were celebrated when they first appeared.

The suggestion that a poet needs to hold some conception of his audience has been variously put aside in more recent years, largely because in recent years poets have lost their audience. Rilke addressed his angels and Day Lewis has said the poet writes for himself. The idea that the poet should, in the normal state of things, write for other people – as many as will listen – has been forgotten, and in any case will not help the poet. Today it is probably impossible to say who reads verse; there is no 'body' of verse-readers, and the receptive, co-operative state of mind which constitutes a 'living audience' for poetry only occurs in individuals. Consequently the poet has little idea for whom he writes. But I am sure that such an idea is a desirable condition for the poet – he can never be certain of himself as an audience and the angels may not care for verse. This is not to say that the poet cannot write well for perhaps half-a-dozen acquaintances whom he respects; it is difficult to generalize about this because we are always being surprised by the conditions under which a poet may write well if he is able to do so at all. Where narrative poetry is concerned, though, I feel it to be not only a desirable condition but also essential that the poet shall have some conception of his audience. Perhaps this sense of an audience is not entirely a social question; perhaps it is something in the poet's nature which makes him envisage an audience – abstract, mutable as the vision is. Those poets who write plays have this sense. Masefield has it, and there are few after him, except for recent poet-dramatists who have been able to possess it (i.e. have been given the chance to do so).

But John Masefield has never glorified 'the people' as an audience – 'People listen to stories, because life is so prone to action that the very shadow of action will sway the minds of men and women: any purpose will arrest no purpose,'[1] he

[1] *Chaucer (Recent Prose).*

has said. And, in the preface to his book on Shakespeare (written about the time of *The Everlasting Mercy*), when he was speaking of the lack of an adequate theatre in London for the production of Shakespeare's plays, he wrote: 'They (the millions) pass from one grey street to another grey street, to add up figures, or to swallow patent medicines, with no thought that life has been lived nobly, and burningly and knightly, for great ends, and in great passions. . . .'[1]

I am dealing in the following chapters with three of Masefield's numerous narrative poems: *The Everlasting Mercy*, *Dauber*, and *Reynard the Fox*. In *The Widow in the Bye Street* there occur fine passages, but I do not think the poem as a whole can refute the charge of sentimentality. It is a dreadfully depressing piece. *Right Royal* is well worth the reader's attention for the scene of the horse-race alone; the rhythm is remarkable. But its theme does not grip as does that of *Reynard*. Many good verses are to be found in *The Daffodil Fields* – an excellent story which might have been better told in prose. In particular I would draw attention to *Minnie Maylow's Story* – a humorous, entertaining piece; the number of ways in which Masefield has contrived to describe a locust is a rare feat of ingenuity.

The narrative *King Cole* has the rich and lively background of circus life but, like his poems on the Arthurian legend, it lacks the immediacy of feeling and theme which mark the three poems I propose to examine in the following pages.

These three poems are, I think, his best. They are also, in different ways, representative of the poet's narrative art as a whole.

---

[1]*Shakespeare* (1911).

Five

'The Everlasting Mercy'

I

Masefield has written a retrospective account of how *The Everlasting Mercy* came into being. It was after a period of dejection, frustration and difficulties with his literary work; after a period when 'the work seemed in a tangle, and not to be cleared by any effort of mine'. He took his work away, alone, to another part of the country 'working and worrying for a few days, finding no light upon it, yet sure that the promised light would come'. During an evening walk in May through wooded countryside he had an experience of profound and joyful response to the beauty of the spring woodlands opening around him. 'I was in a state of great inner joy from a sight I had seen that morning,' he writes, linking the present sensations with an earlier one. 'I came home uphill through a wood, feeling that the incredible and the impossible were on each side of me. At the wood's edge there was a sort of fence to shut it from the common beyond. The fence was something to step over with the feet, and easily to push through with the body. As I went over and through this division, I said to myself, "Now I will make a poem about a blackguard who becomes converted." Instantly the poem appeared to me in its complete form, with every detail distinct; the opening lines poured out upon the page as fast as I could write them down.'[1]

[1] *So Long to Learn.*

Feeling that every word of this account is significant in relation to the form the poem was to take, and that it also bears a general significance to the nature of inspiration, I propose to examine the statement closely. I think it is easy to recognize in the moment of illumination which every artist experiences at times, a kinship with that primitive order of religious revelation which is described in *The Everlasting Mercy*. These are the moments which Shelley, in his Platonic way, declared could never be expressed in their entirety: – the most perfect poem would be but a shadow, and which Proust describes as connecting with an earlier experience in a quite illogical way which can only be described as mystical. When Masefield writes, 'I was in a state of great inner joy from a sight I had seen that morning', he asserts the dual aspect of the moment of inspiration, and as with Proust (in the incident of stumbling on the cobbles of the Guermantes courtyard), John Masefield at that moment saw the world around him as a new, a real and felicitous reality. 'I came home . . . feeling that the incredible and the impossible were on each side of me.' That is the paradox of inspiration – the incredible and the impossible are felt to be present and therefore (for what is more actual than what we feel?) are credible and possible.

If such an experience, a mystical revelation, is 'unutterable',[1] if the inspiration itself cannot be conveyed, the work of art which is its flower will probably spring where the seed is sown. The poem will have an organic connection with its physical origin, and the pattern of events and their movement at the visionary instant will be translated symbolically until in the end the work itself becomes the real thing and the events the symbols of it. Thus, one may find the story of Saul Kane's conversion repeated in the details given by Masefield, of the exact moment at which he said, 'Now I will make a poem about a blackguard who becomes converted.' The

---

[1]*'What can be revealed cannot be uttered'* (Wittgenstein).

poet has come uphill through a wood. At the wood's edge there is 'a sort of fence to shut it from the common beyond'.

This is the pattern of an uphill journey through the wood's darkness into the light at the edge of the wood where, however, there is a barrier to separate the traveller from common ground. Similarly, Saul Kane's spiritual journey, uphill through the darkness of sin, ends only when he has crossed the fence (of faith) into the 'common' (the place of salvation common to all men). 'The fence was something to step over with the feet, and easily to push through with the body,' writes Masefield. There is a tremendous sense of the physical in Saul Kane's conversion. The poet does not make him a 'higher being' in the sense that he is at all a man of thought. Saul Kane is a most physical being, he is nearly all body; the barrier of faith to the thoughtful or intellectually developed being is an intellectual one. To Saul Kane that could never be the case, the barrier would have to be a physical one, and this is difficult for people with even a small degree of literacy to understand.

In his nineteenth-century revivalist setting, in his rustic illiteracy, the character of Saul Kane's conversion is psychologically right – the acceptance of Christ to such a man would not rest on the result of a conflict between reason and feeling (as does the type of religious conflict most easily recognized by readers of poetry and hence by those who are most likely to misunderstand *The Everlasting Mercy*). Saul Kane's conversion needs must rest, as it does, in the outcome of a conflict between body and soul. This character is symbolized by, and was conceived in, the poet's simple and otherwise insignificant action of stepping over a fence which, however, we are told explicitly, 'was something to step over with the feet, and easily to push through with the body'. The feet, which connect the body with the earth, and the body itself, must be able to get through 'this division' before Saul Kane is converted.

They were wrong who suggested that Saul Kane's experience was Masefield's own. The poet's experience was an artistic one – a period of darkness and difficulty leading to the edge of light and meaning, culminating with the inspiration received on his spring-time walk, and all this, too, has no doubt a symbolic association with the general outline of Saul Kane's story. But the form of *The Everlasting Mercy*, the form which appeared to the poet complete, with every detail distinct just as he was getting through the fence, follows, I feel, the pattern of those apparently simple and trifling incidents which took place at the inspired instant. It may be that inspiration is a power which travels faster than light, sound, touch or any other medium of the senses; that this force strikes first, and in the case of the artist, seizes on whatever random objects and events lie at hand, presenting them in a unified form for the purpose of fulfilment. Sometimes the work of art will proceed directly from this conglomerate pattern, but most often it will be translated by the artist into a unity, symbolic of its original, and un-recognizable from it, unless we are fortunate enough to be told, as Masefield has told us, what trivial and un-momentous doings the artist was about when the inspiration descended.

II

One can well believe that the opening lines of *The Everlasting Mercy* 'poured out upon the page' as fast as the poet could write them. Their unusual merits and unusual defects combine in almost careless rapture:

> From '41 to '51
> I was my folk's contrary son;
> I bit my father's hand right through
> And broke my mother's heart in two.
> I sometimes go without my dinner
> Now that I know the times I've gi'n her.

From '51 to '61
I cut my teeth and took to fun.
I learned what not to be afraid of
And what stuff women's lips are made of;
I learned with what a rosy feeling
Good ale makes floors seem like the ceiling,
And how the moon gives shiny light
To lads as roll home singing by't.
My blood did leap, my flesh did revel,
Saul Kane was tokened to the devil.

From '61 to '67
I lived in disbelief of heaven,
I drunk, I fought, I poached, I whored,
I did despite unto the Lord,
I cursed, 'twould make a man look pale,
And nineteen times I went to jail.
   Now, friends, observe and look upon me,
   Mark how the Lord took pity on me.

It must be remembered that this is the speech of a rustic. Not that any serious poet would produce rustic speech *verbatim* in verse; it would sound fake. To be convincing such effects have, in fact, to be faked a little, and faking is part of a poet's job. When Wordsworth in his Preface to *Lyrical Ballads* spoke of the 'language really used by men' and 'the very language of men' he was speaking of the language used by rustics, and this waylaid Coleridge who, seeing a flaw in the theory, substituted his *lingua communis*. Now rustics do not speak in the *lingua communis*, though the phrase was apt enough for Wordsworth's verse, which was the speech of Wordsworth.

Especially does a narrative or dramatic poem need 'the language really used by men' – 'the very language of men' – but with the qualification that it must be the language of the men who are portrayed in the poem. They should speak, or should be spoken of, in a 'common tongue' which is, however, particularly adapted to the environment the poet has created for them. Any poet who tackles this problem (it is every poet's problem) needs a strong faculty for analysing words and phrases. Neither Wordsworth nor Masefield possess this; consequently when they succeed they are both apt to write something very fine, and when they fail, very funny.

I cannot, for example, conceive any time in history when the lines

> I sometimes go without my dinner
> Now that I know the times I've gi'n her

will sound other than comic. For one thing, Saul Kane's repentance at 'the times' (a good colloquialism in itself) he has given his mother, has the same effect on him as would a piece of bad fish, and this, though likely, is droll. Secondly, 'gi'n her' and 'dinner' are poor rhymes; and when the skill of the artist is not equal to his subject, the consequent incongruity throws doubt on the sincerity of the subject. (We all know funny verses on subjects of piety or love written with the sincerest feelings by people without poetic skill. I am against the idea that a poet's sincerity can be measured by his intention. He is the sincerest poet, perhaps, who tries to show off, to do something as near-perfect as possible with entire surrender to his effect, with the concentration which we expect of a good trapeze acrobat.)

We must remember always that Masefield's first aim is to tell a story: that his aim is first to arouse interest, then to sustain it, lastly to satisfy it. Consistently bad verse will of course defeat this aim; but John Masefield's verse is not bad, it is inconsistent. You get good and bad in extremes, most often in the same poem, all through his work. Yet in many cases the details are overwhelmed, good and bad alike, by the powerful conception and the skilful shape of the work.

Look again at the lines I have quoted which open *The Everlasting Mercy*. They arouse interest. This is due partly to the rhythm; that alone has an Evangelical-Revivalist beat – full of an earthy kind of joy. Then there are lines like

> My blood did leap, my flesh did revel,
> Saul Kane was tokened to the devil.

The language of revivalist confession is here; the lines come
pouring out in the excited rhythms proper to that flesh and
blood which are 'tokened to the devil' – rhythms the opposite
of liturgical. The name Saul Kane has a self-apparent
Biblical connotation, but at the same time it places the man
in that society of God-fearing rustic folk who were accustomed to give their children Biblical names. We learn
immediately that he was born of such stock in 1841, grew to
be a wild lawless youth, and found his salvation in the year
1867. The story is Saul Kane's account of the events leading
up to his conversion; and as it is given from a post-
conversion standpoint, his tale takes on two aspects of
Revivalist expression: the unsparing and open confession,
and the admonitory exhortation. Saul Kane is both con-
fessant and preacher.

> Now, friends, observe and look upon me,
> Mark how the Lord took pity on me.

Such interjections recur throughout the narrative with the
effect that while the course of the tale is unfolded incident by
incident, we are always being reminded that the narrator is
newly-saved. It is a story of sin and salvation, in which sin is
shown as acting as a fertilizer on the spirit – evil was to Saul
Kane's conversion as dung to the harvest; and this process is
essentially of Revivalism. Now parodists and other critics of
The Everlasting Mercy have tacitly and openly posited the
question: is Saul Kane worth writing about? This is always a
legitimate question: one which Aristotle raised. Aesthetically, the question is, did Saul Kane sin *sufficiently* to warrant
his conversion: were his drunkenness, whoring and other
local crimes, for which he nineteen times went to jail, of
sufficient universal magnitude to call forth his tremendous
and lyrical change of heart? Morally, the question does not

arise; a sense of original sin in a comparatively blameless man might have the same effect. But in an art which deals with concrete factors, which is not philosophical, and above all with narrative art, the question is very pertinent.

E.V. Knox, in a parody, answered this question in his own way

> I used to be a fearful lad,
> The things I did were downright bad;

and goes on to describe 'the Everlasting Percy', travelling on trains without a ticket, underneath the seat, smoking in 'non-smokers', pulling the communication-cord, and other bits of wickedness committed 'from sinfulness and shameful pride'. John Squire felt much the same way about Masefield's work, and was, I think, both justified and successful where he mimics the technical faults.

Before we can answer the question, we have to be sure what Saul Kane's 'sins' were. 'I drunk, I fought, I poached, I whored' – these are all elaborated in the narrative in detail; added to this, in a mood of mad revolt against the sanctimonious respectability of his village he embarks on a wild night escapade, running naked through the streets, ringing the fire-bell, breaking windows, banging on doors. If this series of actions represents the source of Saul Kane's guilt which led to his salvation, I would agree that so far as the work of art is concerned, the cause does not balance the effect. Simply as a village nuisance, Saul Kane is not evil enough, and as such his nineteen visits to jail do him sufficient justice. But the poem gives a profounder and a universal source of guilt which was the turning-point in Saul Kane's career. It is recounted in the first phase of the story, and I think entirely justifies the sequence of events.

The story opens with Saul Kane in the act of poaching on territory which 'belongs', by a mutual arrangement, to another poacher. He is approached and challenged by his

friend, and Kane, who knows very well the field is not 'his',
claims it.

> He tells me 'Get to hell from there.
> This field is mine,' he says, 'by right;
> If you poach here, there'll be a fight.
> Out now,' he says, 'and leave your wire;
> It's mine.'
>   'It ain't.'
>   'You put.'
>   'You liar.'
> 'You closhy put.'
>   'You bloody liar.'
> 'This is my field.'
>   'This is my wire.'
> 'I'm ruler here.'
>   'You ain't.'
>   'I am.'
> 'I'll fight you for it.'
>   'Right, by damn.'

It should be noted that the rights and wrongs of poaching are
not here in question; the offence is not against property but
against honour. And Saul Kane's protracted persistence in
this offence is the origin of his sense of guilt and subsequent
salvation. The lines continue:

> Those were the words, that was the place
> By which God brought me into grace.

I consider, then, that the reader's sympathies are engaged in
a cause of proper magnitude, and this is clear if the poem is
read aright. It is the cause of honour among thieves, if you
will, but it is equally true that *Macbeth* treats of honour
among tyrants. The serious, because permanent, factor is
honour. It is because Saul Kane transgresses a universal, not
a local, law, that his repentance is aesthetically acceptable.
And so, I think, is the tone of the poem – that is, the mode of

expression, the issues which are emphasized; the attitude. All are appropriate to an unsophisticated elemental setting: the society of which Saul Kane is a member; all are appropriate to nineteenth-century Evangelicalism in country districts.

Psychologically, the course of the narrative which is the course of Kane's spiritual development is sound. I would like to trace the story from this aspect; noting also the effects the poet is out to make; where he achieves them and where he fails. Before doing so, I would remark that it is imperative for a proper understanding of the poem to read it whole. It is the wholeness that really counts. No part is any indication of the total effect. The following summary and analysis is intended to indicate in what particulars the essence of the whole is realized; for the parts frequently epitomize the whole.

The time comes round for the fight. Supporters of both sides have placed their bets and gather round. Kane has a moment's hesitation:

> I thought how long we two'd been friends,
> And in my mind, about that wire,
> I thought, 'He's right, I am a liar.
>
> . . . .
>
> I'm fighting to defend a lie.
> And this moonshiny evening's fun
> Is worse than aught I ever done.'
> And thinking that way my heart bled so
> I almost stept to Bill and said so.

But Kane, on the verge of owning his lie, remembers his friends in the crowd who have placed bets on him. The preparations continue. Before the fight starts, Kane has a second revulsion:

> And looking round I felt a spite,
> At all who'd come to see me fight;

95

drunkards and louts who had never themselves engaged in anything but a brawl. And once more before the fight begins Kane is moved to make amends:

> I thought 'I'll go and take Bill's hand.
> I'll up and say the fault was mine,
> He sha'n't make play for these here swine.'
> And then I thought that that was silly,
> They'd think I was afraid of Billy:
> They'd think (I thought it, God forgive me)
> I funked the hiding Bill could give me.
> And that thought made me mad and hot.
> 'Think that, will they? Well, they shall not.
> They sha'n't think that. I will not. I'm
> Damned if I will. I will not.'
>
> Time!

Up to this point Masefield has been concentrating on his hero's situation. When he comes to the episode of the fight, he does something which is happily characteristic of all his work: he digresses without losing sight of his central theme. He digresses here to follow the fight in close and exciting detail, but it is not a diversion from the subject, for the men are very much present in each line. Chaucer has something of this method, but his digressions, the *Tales*, are not apparently of the one theme; they are separate. The classics of this method are Homer and Virgil. The method is of the epic though, of course, the work in question is not an epic.

To make clear what I think Masefield has uniquely attempted to do, I must say something here about his method in relation to other narrative types.

The Border Ballads are concerned with the lyrical winding in and out of a situation; for all their repetitiveness and length, they are models of narrative economy. For, in the Border Ballads, we get a 'compiled' narrative – a sequence of events stated in such a way that they have the power to suggest what is left unsaid, the logical connections. In one

verse the lover (let us say) is with his lady; in the next he has
run to his mother's bower, or is sailing the seas. There is no
dissipation of imagery – no indication of the route to the
mother's bower, whether it took three minutes, three hours
or three days – no digression about the getting of the ship,
where it was built, the launching of it. This is a process
peculiar to the Border Ballad construction. For example I
choose at random the following:

> He felt nae pity for Lillie Flower
> > Where she was lying dead;
> But he felt some for the bonny bairn
> > That lay weltering in her bluid.
>
> Up has he ta'en that bonny boy,
> > Given him to nurses nine;
> Three to sleep, and three to wake,
> > And three to go between.
>
> And he bred up that bonny boy,
> > Call's him his sister's son;
> And he thought nae eye could ever see
> > The deed that had been done.

Here is a complete situation in twelve lines, presented with
perfect clarity. The whole story of the child's birth and
upbringing is conveyed by substitution of parts. For
example, the two lines 'Three to sleep, and three to wake, /
And three to go between' are not merely decorative; they
serve the function of informing us with what vigilance the
child was cared for – amid what substance and wealth, on
which Homer might have descanted for a hundred lines and
more.

John Masefield's narrative style, however, is in the
episodic manner; he places story within story, and these
digressions are at their best curiously representative of the
larger theme. It is also akin to Sir Walter Scott's narrative
verse. Scott, like Masefield, takes his time. Scott, on the

other hand, is more of the novelist-as-poet; he gets his characters fixed in his readers' minds by telling us, roughly, their background and what they are wearing; then, Scott has a plot which transcends these characters. Masefield has a story, not a plot. And this is because his characters seem to make the story. His characters are furthermore established in our minds by what they do as well as how they look. Scott's view of men is historical, Masefield's is social.

To return to *The Everlasting Mercy*; the fight presents an excellent opportunity to digress, which the poet seizes. He makes very exciting work of it.

> 'Get up,' cried Jim. I said, 'I will.'
> Then all the gang yelled, 'Out him, Bill.
> Out him.' Bill rushed . . . and Clink, Clink, Clink.
> Time! And Jim's knee, and rum to drink.
> And round the ring there ran a titter:
> 'Saved by the call, the bloody quitter.'
>
> They drove (a dodge that never fails)
> A pin beneath my finger nails.
> They poured what seemed a running beck
> Of cold spring water down my neck;
>
>   . . . .
> Time!
>   There was Bill as grim as death.
> He rushed, I clinched, to get more breath
> And breath I got, though Billy bats
> Some stinging short-arms in my slats.

Things go badly for Kane until Bill's thumb, not quite mended from a recent sprain, gives way again. Kane knows that the fight is his, but it takes him five more rounds to put Bill out.

> With all his skill and all his might
> He clipped me dizzy left and right;
> The Lord knows what the effort cost,

There follows a realistic account of Bill's pain. Of all things, physical pain is the most difficult to describe, because in its real acuteness it is not easily imagined. The poet here gets very close to the actual thing:

> . . . if you'd like to feel his pain,
> You sprain your thumb and hit the sprain,
> And hit it hard, with all your power
> On something hard for half an hour,
> While someone thumps you black and blue,
> And then you'll know what Billy knew.

Saul Kane wins the day and his backers take him off in triumph to the 'Lion'. The scene at the 'Lion' is one of the best in the poem, and it gains force from the fact that it does not follow immediately after the fight scene. There is a pause in the action after the fight to allow Kane to speak in his post-salvation mood. This passage is one in which the more intense type of poetry has its proper place, coming with a sort of mounting rhythmic fervour between a scene of violence and a scene of debauch. It describes what Kane observed on the way to the 'Lion'.

> A dog barked, and an owl was calling,
> The Squire's brook was still a-falling,
> The carved heads on the church looked down
> On 'Russell, Blacksmith of this Town',
> And all the graves of all the ghosts
> Who rise on Christmas Eve in hosts
> To dance and carol in festivity
> For joy of Jesus Christ's Nativity
> (Bell-ringer Dawe and his two sons
> Beheld 'em from the bell-tower once),
> Two and two about about
> Singing the end of Advent out,
> Dwindling down to windlestraws
> When the glittering peacock craws,
> As craw the glittering peacock should

When Christ's own star comes over the wood.
Lamb of the sky come out of fold
Wandering windy heavens cold.
- So they shone and sang till twelve
When all the bells ring out of theirselve;
Rang a peal for Christmas morn,
Glory, men, for Christ is born.

There is something, next, of an apocalyptic vision as Kane sees (as did Ringer Dawe mentioned above) the ghostly congregation of the past:

Faces at the window dark
Crowding, crowding, row on row,
Till all the church began to glow.
The chapel glowed, the nave, the choir,
All the faces became fire
Below the eastern window high
To see Christ's star come up the sky.
Then they lifted hands and turned,
And all their lifted fingers burned,
Burned like the golden altar tallows,
Burned like a troop of God's own Hallows,
Bringing to mind the burning time
When all the bells will rock and chime
And burning saints on burning horses
Will sweep the planets from their courses
And loose the stars to burn up night.
Lord, give us eyes to bear the light.

Whereupon the narrative, in its lower key, is resumed:

We all went quiet down the Scallenge
Lest Police Inspector Drew should challenge.

The pub scene (which so scandalized a section of the public in 1911) is chiefly remarkable for the technical achievement of dialogue such as this between Doxy Jane and Saul Kane:

I blew out lamp 'fore she could speak.
She said, 'If you ain't got a cheek,'
And then beside me in the dim,
'Did he beat you or you beat him?'
'Why, I beat him' (though that was wrong),
She said, 'You must be turble strong.
I'd be afraid you'd beat me, too.'
'You'd not,' I said, 'I wouldn't do.'
'Never?'
   'No, never.'
    'Never?'
     'No.'
'O Saul, Here's missus. Let me go.'

It is at about this point that Kane's real sin is usually lost sight of, and identified with the carry-on of himself and his cronies at the pub. The crude debauchery is, however, nothing more than the aura surrounding the nucleus of his guilt. The essential thing is still the lie which he has successfully defended; which the parodists miss by concentrating on purely atmospheric passages like:

Jim Gurvil said his smutty say
About a girl down Bye Street way.
And how the girl from Frogatt's circus
Died giving birth in Newent work'us.
And Dick told how the Dymock wench
Bore twins, poor thing, on Dog Hill bench;
And how he'd owned to one in court

Passages like this build up the story; they give Kane his background and represent the darkness from which he is presently to revolt. The language of misanthropy is not far off. (Note for instance, in the next verse the lines

And in a slum the reeking hag
Mumbles a crust with toothy jag,

reminiscent of Swift.)

101

And again, it is the management of dialogue which makes vivid the passage where the party reaches its maudlin stage:

> From drunken man to drunken man
> The drunken madness raged and ran.
> 'I'm climber Joe who climbed the spire.'
> 'You're climber Joe the bloody liar.'
> 'Who says I lie?'
>   'I do.'
>   'You lie,
> I climbed the spire and had a fly.'
> 'I'm French Suzanne, the Circus Dancer,
> I'm going to dance a bloody Lancer.'
> 'If I'd my rights I'm Squire's heir.'
> 'By rights I'd be a millionaire.'
> 'By rights I'd be the lord of you,
> But Farmer Scriggins had his do,
> He done me, so I've had to hoove it,
> I've got it all wrote down to prove it.'

When the house falls into a drunken sleep, Kane is overtaken by a second revulsion. He leans out of the window. Again the motif of Grace is introduced.

> The clock struck three, and sweetly, slowly,
> The bells chimed Holy, Holy, Holy;
> And in a second's pause there fell
> The cold note of the chapel bell,

Overwhelmed by the meaninglessness of his existence he is tempted to throw himself down.

> 'Why not?' said I. 'Why not? But no,
> I won't. I've never had my go.
> I've not had all the world can give.
> Death by and by, but first I'll live.'

His next reaction is revolt against the small-town hypocrisy of which he has a sudden and clear vision.

'I'll tell this sanctimonious crowd,
This town of window-peeping, prying,
Maligning, peering, hinting, lying,
Male and female human blots
Who would but daren't be, whores and sots,
That they're so steeped in petty vice
That they're less excellent than lice
That they're so soaked in petty virtue
That touching one of them will dirt you,
Dirt you with the stain of mean
Cheating trade and going between,
Pinching, starving, scraping, hoarding,
Spying through the chinks of boarding
To see if Sue the prentice lean
Dares to touch the margarine.

The scene of Saul Kane's madness[1] is one of the high spots of
the poem, both from the psychological and the descriptive
points of view. Kane strips and flings his clothes, his boots,
the punch-bowl and the drinking-mugs through the window,
shattering the glass. He runs naked into the street; he makes
for the fire-bell screaming that he is Satan.

I've been a ringer, so I know
How best to make a big bell go.
So on to bell-rope swift I swoop,
And stick my one foot in the loop
And heave a down-swing till I groan,
'Awake, you swine, you devil's own.'

As the bell rings out, and the town wakes and panic spreads,
the tempo of the verse is increased by virtue of the lines being
more densely-worded, more alliterative than in the looser lines
of dialogue. Note, in the following, how the poet moulds the
element of sound into a large, amorphous shape, progressively
gaining concrete form, in the fine metaphor of the bird.

[1] Masefield himself gave the title 'Saul Kane's Madness' to this passage,
reprinted in his *Book of Both Sorts*.

103

I felt the air mingle and clang
And beat the walls a muffled bang,
And stifle back and boom and bay
Like muffled peals on Boxing Day,
And then surge up and gather shape,
And spread great pinions and escape;
And each great bird of clanging shrieks
O Fire, Fire! from iron beaks.

The ensuing chaotic conversation between the firemen, the muddled debate as to where the fire is, gives point to Kane's mad utterance, method to his madness.

'I am the fire. Back, stand back,
Or else I'll fetch your skulls a crack;
D'you see these copper nozzles here?
They weigh ten pounds apiece, my dear;
I'm fire of hell come up this minute
To burn this town, and all that's in it.
To burn you dead and burn you clean,
You cogwheels in a stopped machine,
Your hearts of snakes, and brains of pigeons
You dead devout of dead religions,
You offspring of the hen and ass,
By Pilate ruled, and Caiaphas.
Now your account is totted. Learn
Hell's flames are loose and you shall burn.'

The lines achieve an effect of speed, where the befuddled firemen pursue Kane blindly through the autumn night, with Kane banging the nozzles of a couple of fire-hoses on every door. One piece here has a touch of Blake, both in style and thought:

But parson's glass I spared a tittle.
He gave me an orange once when little,
And he who gives a child a treat
Makes joy-bells ring in Heaven's street.

And he who gives a child a home
Builds palaces in Kingdom come,
And she who gives a baby birth
Brings Saviour Christ again to Earth,
For life is joy, and mind is fruit,
And body's precious earth and root.

Kane's inevitable hang-over, in both the spiritual and physical sense, occurs next day; to be followed by, after he has gathered strength, a second 'madness'.

'The second trumpet shall be blown.
The second trump, the second blast;
Hell's flames are loosed, and judgment's passed
Too late for mercy now. Take warning
I'm death and hell and Judgment morning.'

As a picture of the popular radical reasoning of the times, which led sometimes to social revolt, sometimes to Evangelicalism, Kane's encounter, while his 'second madness' was upon him, with the parson, is of some account. 'The police,' says the parson – seeming to summon a host of temporal Powers to his cause, in that one phrase –

'The police will deal with you, my man.'
'Not yet,' said I, 'not yet they won't;
And now you'll hear me, like or don't.
The English Church both is and was
A subsidy of Caiaphas.
I don't believe in Prayer nor Bible,
They're lies all through, and you're a libel,
A libel on the Devil's plan
When first he miscreated man.
You mumble through a formal code
To get which martyrs burned and glowed.
I look on martyrs as mistakes,
But still they burned for it at stakes;

105

Your only fire's the jolly fire
Where you can guzzle port with Squire,'

and,

'You teach the ground-down starving man
That Squire's greed's Jehovah's plan.
You get his learning circumvented
Lest it should make him discontented
(Better a brutal, starving nation
Than men with thoughts above their station),
You let him neither read nor think,
You goad his wretched soul to drink
And then to jail, the drunken boor;
O sad intemperance of the poor.
You starve his soul till it's rapscallion,
Then blame his flesh for being stallion.
You send your wife around to paint
The golden glories of "restraint".
How moral exercise bewild'rin
Would soon result in fewer children.
You work a day in Squire's fields
And see what sweet restraint it yields;
A woman's day at turnip picking,
Your heart's too fat for plough or ricking.'

to which the parson replies,

'You think that Squire and I are kings
Who made the existing state of things,
And made it ill. I answer, No,
States are not made, nor patched; they grow,
Grow slow through centuries of pain
And grow correctly in the main,
But only grow by certain laws
Of certain bits in certain jaws.
You want to doctor that. Let be.
You cannot patch a growing tree.
Put these two words beneath your hat,

These two: securus judicat.
The social states of human kinds
Are made by multitudes of minds,
And after multitudes of years
A little human growth appears
Worth having, even to the soul
Who sees most plain it's not the whole.
This state is dull and evil, both,
I keep it in the path of growth;
You think the Church an outworn retter;
Kane, keep it, till you've built a better.
And keep the existing social state;
I quite agree it's out of date,
One does too much, another shirks,
Unjust, I grant; but still . . . it works.
To get the whole world out of bed
And washed, and dressed, and warmed, and fed,
To work, and back to bed again,
Believe me, Saul, costs worlds of pain.
Then, as to whether true or sham
That book of Christ, Whose priest I am;
The Bible is a lie, say you,
Where do you stand, suppose it true?
Good-bye. But if you've more to say,
My doors are open night and day.
Meanwhile, my friend, 'twould be no sin
To mix more water in your gin.
We're neither saints nor Philip Sidneys,
But mortal men with mortal kidneys.'
He took his snuff, and wheezed a greeting,
And waddled off to mothers' meeting;

The thing to be noted about this dialogue is not of course the
dialectical skill or originality of either party, but the very
opposite, its typical quality. It is altogether the sort of thing
such a young man as Saul Kane would justifiably say – just
the sort of thing such a rural vicar would reply.

As evening approaches Kane, having fortified himself at
the 'Lion', is waiting about for his girl who fails to turn up. At

this point the poet introduces one of those most suitable purple splashes which act as a preparation for something momentous about to come, so that the later episode will not be too abrupt. As Kane loiters on the country road, an apocalyptic change comes over the elements: his senses are on edge; he is alert to slight movements and sounds and sensitive to the wind in his face. This passage, quoted below, can be taken both as an experience in which nature prefigures the coming change in Kane's soul, and as a description of a change in the weather. In both senses, the lines are extremely evocative; the plain, casual verse slips very easily into the poetic:

> The moon come pale, the wind come cool,
> A big pike leapt in Lower Pool,
> The peacock screamed, the clouds were straking,
> My cut cheek felt the weather breaking;
> An orange sunset waned and thinned
> Foretelling rain and western wind,
> And while I watched I heard distinct
> The metals on the railway clinked.
> The blood-edged clouds were all in tatters,
> The sky and earth seemed mad as hatters;
> They had a death look, wild and odd,
> Of something dark foretold by God.
> And seeing it so, I felt so shaken
> I wouldn't keep the road I'd taken
> But wandered back towards the inn
> Resolved to brace myself with gin.
> And as I walked, I said, 'It's strange,
> There's Death let loose to-night, and Change.'

'The peacock screamed' has a strange effect. Why did the poet bring a peacock, of all birds, into this English rural (probably West Midlands) scene? – except for the purpose of intensifying the new, rather alien, rich and exotic emanation which Kane had briefly sensed. These lines pick up the earlier passage where Kane speaks of the phantom choristers

'Dwindling down to windlestraws / When the glittering peacock craws' (see p. 99). The possible allusions are many. We are, perhaps, referred to some superstition or legend, or to the 'golden bird' that tops the spire of Ledbury Church; which fabulous creature, it is supposed, has come alive to prophesy 'Death let loose to-night' – death of the old Kane, that is; 'and Change' – his conversion. Or this peacock, it may be, is a rare, a greatly prized show-bird, the property of the Squire, strutting about some private park and emulating, for one famous moment of its life, the cock which St Peter heard. The image of the peacock calls up many meanings. The word 'peacock' is full of value, but the bird itself is real enough. Here, if anywhere, we can see where realism differs from and transcends the mere lifelike. The poet's departure from the lifelike is excellently placed.

The scene which follows this is, in my view, irredeemably bad, if not nauseating. How Masefield came to write it, I do not know, except that this is just what he does do at times. Kane has found a small boy crying outside a shop, having lost sight of his mother who is inside. Kane entertains the child with stories; the mother is fetched and, horrified at seeing her child with a well-known bad-lad, treats him to a tirade nearly five pages long. In the course of this speech, her whole family history is hurled forth.

> 'For I've had eight, and buried five,
> And only three are left alive.
> I've given them all we could afford,
> I've taught them all to fear the Lord.
> . . . .
> 'For Minnie whom I loved the worst
> Died mad in childbed with her first.
> And John and Mary died of measles,
> And Rob was drownded at the Teasels.
> And little Nan, dear little sweet,
> A cart run over in the street;
> . . . .
> For Susan went the ways of shame'

And so on, to what purpose in relation to the story it is difficult to see. For the really successful digression (such as the fight scene) is connected symbolically with the story. Not so this episode. The mother's anxiety that her little Jimmy shall not be smirched by Kane's company is made quite clear, but the episode is quite extraneous to the story of Saul Kane's conversion. True, it is said to fill him with shame, but this is not convincing. The woman's prolonged hysteria was more likely to send him back to his pub friends. This scene is a lapse in judgment, where the previous pub scene is not. Only one interesting episode redeems this passage. The story with which Kane entertains little Jimmy anticipates the delightful tom-cat frolics in Masefield's children's classic *The Midnight Folk* – published ten years later. The cat will be recognized, who

> . . . with clever paw,
> Unhooks a broke-brick's secret door:
> Then down into the cellar black,
> Across the wood slug's slimy track,
> Into an old cask's quiet hollow,
> Where they've got seats for what's to follow;
> Then each tom-cat lights little candles,
> And O, the stories and the scandals,
> And O, the songs and Christmas carols,
> And O, the milk from little barrels.

After his encounter with Jimmy's mother, Kane, understandably, returns to revive his spirits at the pub.

> 'Come on, drinks round, salue, drink hearty.
> Now, Jane, the punch-bowl for the party.
> If any here won't drink with me
> I'll knock his bloody eyes out. See?
> Come on, cigars round, rum for mine,
> Sing us a smutty song, some swine.'

and when the missionary, 'the Friend', appears,

> So when she come so prim and grey
> I pound the bar and sing, 'Hooray,
> Here's Quaker come to bless and kiss us,
> Come, have a gin and bitters, missus.
> Or maybe Quaker girls so prim
> Would rather start a bloody hymn.
> Now Dick, oblige. A hymn, you swine,
> Pipe up the "Officer of the Line",
> A song to make one's belly ache,
> Or "Nell the Roger at the Wake",
> Or that sweet song, the talk in town,
> "The lady fair and Abel Brown."
> "O, who's that knocking at the door."
> Miss Bourne'll play the music score.'
> The men stood dumb as cattle are,
> They grinned, but thought I'd gone too far,

The circumstances immediately preceding Saul Kane's change of heart – the brief, banal and effective admonition of the missionary, his drink poured out on the floor – are accompanied, once more, by a sharpening of his senses, a new acuteness of observation. The poet shows how, at vital moments, details of sounds and things seem to draw attention to themselves and symbolize the very essence of the situation. Thus,

> . . . 'Tick. Slow. Tick. Slow' went the clock
> She said, 'He waits until you knock.'
>
> . . . .
>
> I heard her clang the 'Lion' door,
> I marked a drink-drop roll to floor;
> It took up scraps of sawdust, flurry
> And crinkled on, a half inch, blurry;
> A drop from my last glass of gin;
> And someone waiting to come in,

The description of Kane's third 'madness' – that is, the
triumphant afflatus of the convert – contains some of the
finest lines in the poem. Kane sees everything around him
transfigured by his new-found sense of glory:

> Out into darkness, out to night,
> My flaring heart gave plenty light,
> So wild it was there was no knowing
> Whether the clouds or stars were blowing;
>
> . . . .
>
> And in my heart the drink unpriced,
> The burning cataracts of Christ.

His moral sense awakened, he sees with new eyes the
familiar objects of the countryside as symbols of good and
evil:

> All earthly things that blessed morning
> Were everlasting joy and warning.
> The gate was Jesus' way made plain
> The mole was Satan foiled again,
> Black blinded Satan snouting way
> Along the red of Adam's clay;
> The mist was error and damnation,
> The lane the road unto salvation,
> Out of the mist into the light;
> O blessed gift of inner sight.
>
> . . . .
>
> A ploughman's voice, a clink of chain,
> Slow hoofs, and harness under strain.
> Up the slow slope a team came bowing,[1]

The stanzas in which it is revealed to Kane that he will
become a ploughman are as fervent and lyrical as a
Methodist hymn. The whole of Kane's life force wells up in a
spontaneous utterance of joy:

[1]Note the effect of slow, uphill strain given by the use of monosyllabic
words and long vowels.

O wet red swathe of earth laid bare,
O truth, O strength, O gleaming share,
O patient eyes that watch the goal,
O ploughman of the sinner's soul.
O Jesus, drive the coulter deep
To plough my living man from sleep.

and in the lines which found such favour with the Nonconformist clergy in 1911:

O Christ who holds the open gate,
O Christ who drives the furrow straight,
O Christ, the plough, O Christ, the laughter
Of holy white birds flying after,
Lo, all my heart's field red and torn,
And thou wilt bring the young green corn
The young green corn divinely springing,
The young green corn for ever singing,
And when the field is fresh and fair
Thy blessed feet shall glitter there.
And we will walk the weeded field,
And tell the golden harvest's yield,
The corn that makes the holy bread
By which the soul of man is fed,
The hold bread, the food unpriced,
Thy everlasting mercy, Christ.

The Everlasting Mercy is a document of a whole epoch in
history. It characterizes the wave of religious revivalism
which spread over rural England from the time of Wesley,
mid-eighteenth century, right through the nineteenth. The
passage quoted above suggests the dominant notes of
Revivalism: immediacy of apprehension akin to that of
Primitive Christianity, and the buoyant impulse of Pan-
theism embraced within a Christian scheme.

At the close of the poem there is a short lyric, different
from the rhythm and style of the poem itself. This I take to be
the poet's own statement, and brings us back to the spring

day when, according to Masefield's later account, *The Everlasting Mercy* was begun. Spring has passed and summer is passing,

> How swift the summer goes,
> Forget-me-not, pink, rose.
> The young grass when I started
> And now the hay is carted,
> And now my song is ended,
> And all the summer spended;
> The blackbird's second brood
> Routs beech-leaves in the wood,
> The pink and rose have speeded,
> Forget-me-not has seeded.
> Only the winds that blew,
> The rain that makes things new,
> The earth that hides things old,
> And blessings manifold.

> O lovely lily clean,
> O lily springing green,
> O lily bursting white,
> Dear lily of delight,
> Spring in my heart agen
> That I may flower to men.

It is the only personal statement in the poem, and this is only assumed by the change of manner from narrative to reflective. And it is personal in another sense: the poet here seems to be speaking for Kane where previously he had let him speak for himself.

I am not concerned (nor apparently had been the poet), with what sect would have claimed Saul Kane for its own. The Church of England parson has, in his way, as much hand in Kane's conversion as did the Quaker missionary; they appear at different points in his development, and each had an effect on him. The spirit of the whole poem is, however, that of Nonconformist Revivalism; and in calling

The Everlasting Mercy a 'document' of this important religious and social event, I am not placing it below the status of a successful poem. No prose account, no list of historical data, could supply the spirit of Revivalism which is inherent in this pulsating rhythm, the Apocalyptic imagery and, above all, in the story itself of *The Everlasting Mercy*.

In tracing the course of the narrative I have emphasized passages which constitute the pattern of Revivalist emotion in its course from sin to salvation. And in depicting the course of development in one individual, the poet shows a profound insight into the psychological shape of Revivalism.

The pattern is sin, followed by revulsion from sin, followed by the 'madness' or state of emotional ferment which is peculiarly associated with Revivalism. A feature of Saul Kane's 'madness' is that it is repeated three times, each accentuated in a different way. The first 'madness', where Kane runs out naked into the street to ring the fire-bell, and is pursued along the country roads, is physical in kind – a violent exuberance of the body. Kane says, at this point in the story:

> O, if you want to know delight,
> Run naked in an autumn night,
> And laugh, as I laughed then, to find
> A running rabble drop behind,

The stress of the second 'madness', during which Kane encounters the parson, falls on his rational powers. (By this of course I do not mean that Kane's mind is at this point unhinged – his whole being, on all three occasions, is in a turbulent state; but to point out that on the second occasion, Kane is galvanized by the new spirit working within him, through the agency of his reason as distinct from his body.) Thus we have Kane's access of articulate speech, his spirited attack on the Church in the radical tub-thumping style.

The final Christian revelation which Kane experiences is emotional:

> . . . in my heart the drink unpriced
> The burning cataracts of Christ.

The sense of joy and glory which transfigures everything around him infuses his third 'madness', which is a newly-experienced refinement of emotion, a 'change of heart'.

In each phase, Kane's 'madness' enables him to apprehend a portion of truth. The first reality is perceived by means of physical freedom; in casting off his clothes and running naked through the night, Kane seems to have cast off the first bonds that tie him to sin. In 'speaking his mind' to the parson, the second reality becomes apparent; his reason is freed from slavishness. The third and final reality is an emotional awakening touched off by his encounter with the Quaker missionary. It is this last which consummates the apprehension of all three realities for Kane, making them a whole truth.

The attainment of Grace in this way is in a more primitive tradition than we commonly find in religious poetry. There is nothing here of 'the dark night of the soul' conflict to be found in the writings of the great Christian mystics. The progress of Kane's soul towards conversion altogether lacks the meditative method; or that of patient reasoning, or that of stoicism and good works. The salvation of Kane is not in the exalted tradition of the devotional poets. It is in the tradition of the Evangelical Revival which came, as in the pattern of Saul Kane's experience, from a reaching out of emotional forces towards Christianity. I have said earlier that Kane's conflict was between body and soul; so was the conflict of the Revivalist masses. Revivalism may be regarded as 'bad taste' by those in whom the conflict, if present at all, is between faith and reason.

Faith is not a question with Saul Kane; it is there from the start. The moral will is in question. But this is beside the point in considering *The Everlasting Mercy* because I do not think it will appeal to readers who are looking for a religious poem; it will appeal to those who look for an historical poem.

Masefield's talent for the historic and epic first came to light here. The poem is an inspired record of a powerful religious movement, typified in the life of one man. It is also a good story.

Six

'Dauber'

About *The Everlasting Mercy* there is something of the blunt, grim, straightforward cause-and-effect statement that we find in *Peter Grimes*. In *Dauber*, the theme is far more complex. It is the tragedy of a sensitive young man who wishes to become an artist; who we are nowhere told is talented enough to justify this desire; who joins a sailing ship's crew hoping to practise painting ships and the sea; who comes safely through the terrors of working aloft through the fearful weather of Cape Horn; and who meets his end during a second, unexpected storm when he slips and falls to the deck.

The essence of the tragedy might at first seem to lie in a blind operation of chance, the act of some futile massive unconscious Fate which, by a casual flick of the finger, hurls the Dauber to his death. But it is not so simple as that.

Henry James has a story, *Owen Wingate*, the theme of which has a revealing note in common with *Dauber* despite the very different background. Owen Wingate, a member of a family highly self-conscious of its military traditions, throws up his army career on conscientious grounds. The question is, as his friends lose no time in making him feel, are his motives untainted with cowardice? Wingate is a sensitive plant if not a poet, and is a reader of verse. His death occurs in the process of 'proving' his courage. The tragic element of the story is the same as that of *Dauber*. It is this: the fatal error of both Wingate and the Dauber was the attempt to justify their existence in a manner alien to them.

Dauber's death is tragic because it is an alien death. It is not natural to him; it is not that death which Rilke calls 'an individual death';[1] it is not the sort of death which Rilke further describes as being carried within us 'as a fruit bears its kernel'. But the fatal error which incurs this unnatural death lies in Dauber's own character, in his divided purpose, so that in a sense he does bear within him the seed of disaster (that is, of a disastrous, not a natural, death).

An idealist, he is yet not clear about his ideals. He wishes to prove himself in the eyes of the crew; he wishes to prove himself, through his painting, in his own eyes. He achieves the first, and does not live to fulfil the second. And his achievement of the crew's approbation is, after all, but a passing thing. A moment after the Dauber's corpse is tipped over the side . . .

> Fair came the falling wind; a seaman said
> The Dauber was a Jonah;. . . .

In reply to a question about the origin of *Dauber*, Masefield told me that the story of Dauber is a true one which he happened to hear and decided to put into verse. He also said that the theme of the poem is that the artist is compelled to obey an inner law of his being, no matter if disaster or death results. I mention this because I am not at all sure that I am entitled to put a different construction on the theme of Dauber from that which the poet intended. Judging simply by the text of the poem, I do not see Dauber as an artist involved in single-minded devotion to an inner law; but as a young man with a leaning towards painting, who has not yet earned the designation of 'artist' and who, in obedience to his obligations as a ship's hand, proves his prowess not as an artist but as a member of the crew.

It is true that the Dauber undertakes this work in order to gain experience for his art:

[1] *The Notebook of Malte Laurids Brigge.*

The fo'c's'les with the men there, dripping wet.
I know the subjects that I want to get.

. . . .

It's not been done, the sea, not yet been done,
From the inside, by one who really knows;

but this is all part of his tragic error – the error of the
romantic artist who believes he must participate in an
experience he wished to express, not merely observe it. The
fallacy ignores the capacity of an artist for vicarious
experience, the fact that the practice of an art is an
occupation which takes up much time, and also the fact that
a dangerous experience might prove fatal.

It is also true that the Dauber's vision is that of the artist,
though he does not live to express it. In an early stage in the
voyage his attitude is conveyed in the lines:

'This is the art I've come for, and am learning,
The sea and ships and men and travelling things.
It is most proud, whatever pain it brings.'

He leaned upon his arm and watched the light
Sliding and fading to the steady roll;
This he would some day paint, the ship at night
And sleeping seamen tired to the soul;
The space below the bunks as black as coal,
Gleams upon chests, upon the unlit lamp,
The ranging door-hook, and the locker clamp.
This he would paint, and that, and all these scenes.

Later, when the storm comes, he is made to reflect:

Death would be better, death, than this long hell
Of mockery and surrender and dismay —
This long defeat of doing nothing well,

Eventually he does do something well: it is an act of
seamanship, not an act of art. It kills both man and artist.

120

I have said earlier that I think *Dauber* will appeal to present-day readers. This is because his situation and tragedy tallies with much present-day experience. The death of the Dauber is merely the end of a tragic sequence, it does not of itself make the tragedy. There is a schism in his make-up which makes the tragedy. His death achieves, proves, nothing; serves no purpose, is negative. In this respect the tragedy of *Dauber* is in the modern tradition. It differs from the tragedy of the Elizabethans in kind (save for *Hamlet*), where the tragic death occurs with a kind of defiant glory, leaving behind the hero's positive imprint. To further the point, I quote R.L. Stevenson because I think the passage contributes well to the argument, although I differ from him:

> Where death is certain, it seems all one from a personal point of view. The man who lost his life against a hen-roost is in the same pickle with him who lost his life against a fortified place of the first order. . . . It was by a hazard that we learned the conduct of the four mariners of the Wager. There was no room for these brave fellows in the boat, and they were left behind upon the island to a certain death. They were soldiers, they said, and knew well enough it was their business to die; and as their comrades pulled away, they stood upon the beach, gave three cheers, and cried 'God bless the King!' Now one or two of those who were in the boat escaped, against all likelihood to tell the story. That was a great thing for us; but surely it cannot, by any possible twisting of human speech, be construed into anything great for the mariners.
>
> (From *Virginibus Puerisque*.)

Now this is very foolish of Stevenson, he should have known better. For the mariners there was greatness in the knowledge that they were to die for a great purpose, and for a purpose proper to their calling. Stevenson applies himself to the wrong sort of situation. I apply his words to the Dauber's death: it cannot be construed into anything great for the *Dauber*. It is a truly tragic death.

121

To appraise the complex merits of *Dauber* we must be aware of what the poet avoids as well as what he does. Except in one passage, the poem lacks sentimentality. The tale is allowed to proceed austerely without comment either direct or implied. On the positive side we find that entire absorption in the telling of the story of which Masefield has the peculiar knack. *Dauber* contains some of the finest poetry he has ever written. I do not find *Dauber* so consummate a work of art as *Reynard the Fox*, but it has passages which the poet has nowhere else surpassed.

II
The Dramatic Construction of 'Dauber'

The action of the poem takes place within the 'little universe' of a sailing ship – that same order of life which Masefield re-created in *Salt Water Ballads*. Two interdependent stories run side by side: that of the Dauber himself and that of the voyage; one bears the theme of inner life and the other the theme of outwardness in which the crew and the ship are fixed quantities motivated by the forces of nature.

The men go about their perennial business, adapting their behaviour only to wind and sea; men to whom the past means a series of anecdotes; the present, the need for work; and the future, a pay-day. These men are not very different from the ship itself; they are the animate part of the ship. As they wilfully destroy the Dauber's paintings, so does the ship destroy the Dauber. The men, the ship, sea, sky and weather make the voyage. The voyage has a life of its own, and Dauber has a life of his own, that is, Dauber is at first actuated by concerns exclusive of the voyage. Dauber's effect on the voyage is nil: the effect of the voyage on Dauber is profound. As the voyage progresses, so is the Dauber's character revealed in a new aspect. Each stage on the journey, every clash between the Dauber and the ship, brings to light a new facet of his nature.

Dauber has been six weeks at sea when the story begins. In status an 'idler' which, according to Masefield's 'Explanations' appended to the poem, means a member of the round-house mess – 'generally consisting of the carpenter, cook, sailmaker, boatswain, painter, etc.'

> His work was what the mate might care to say;
> He mixed red lead in many a boulli tin;
> His dungarees were smeared with paraffin.
> 'Go drown himself' his round-house mates advised him,
> And all hands called him 'Dauber' and despised him.

At this stage, Dauber is presented both as a young man of sensibility beginning to test himself as a painter, and as a rather pathetic nuisance to his shipmates. On the one hand his sensitivity to his chosen subject emerges from such lines as the following, intensified by bright imagery and close-packed diction:

> . . . his busy pencil moved,
> Drawing the leap of water off the side
> Where the great clipper trampled iron-hooved,
> Making the blue hills of the sea divide,
> Shearing a glittering scatter in her stride,
> And leaping on full tilt with all sails drawing,
> Proud as a war-horse, snuffing battle, pawing.

On the other hand, Dauber goes limp, he loses status, when prompt action is needed:

> Down sank the crimson sun into the sea,
> The wind cut chill at once, the west grew dun.
> 'Out sidelights!' called the mate. 'Hi, where is he?'
> The Boatswain called, 'Out sidelights, damn you! Run!'
> 'He's always late or lazing,' murmured one —
> 'The Dauber, with his sketching.'. . .
>
>   .   .   .   .
>
> 'You thing, you twice-laid thing from Port Mahon!'

123

Then came the Cook's 'Is that the Dauber there?
Why don't you leave them stinking paints alone?
They stink the house out, poisoning all the air.
Just take them out.' 'Where to?' 'I don't care where.
I won't have stinking paint here.' From their plates:
'That's right; wet paint breeds fever,' growled his
    mates.

To the reader, Dauber now becomes an object of pity.
Everywhere responsive to beauty, everywhere reviled, his
only consolation is the conviction that he suffers for his art.
Not consolation, but a kind of pain, is the experience of:

Watching the constellations rise and burn,
Until the beauty took him by the throat,
So stately is their glittering overturn;
Armies of marching eyes, armies that yearn
With banners rising and falling, and passing by
Over the empty silence of the sky.

Compensation comes in the form of idealism:

'This is the art I've come for, and am learning,
The sea and ships and men and travelling things.
It is most proud, whatever pain it brings.'

Already he is beginning to dread the voyage, with the
approaching hell of Cape Horn. His position as an artist is
being rendered gradually more helpless. Some of the crew
get hold of his paintings and ruin them.

              'There was six weeks' time
Just wasted in these drawings: it's a crime!'

'Well, don't you say we did it,' growled his mates,
'And as for crime, be damned! the things were smears —
Best overboard, like you, with shot for weights;
Thank God, they're gone, and now go shake your ears.'
The Dauber listened, very near to tears.
'Dauber, if I were you,' said Sam again,
'I'd aft, and see the Captain and complain.'

Dauber, of course, takes Sam at his word and, to the men's delight, goes to complain to the Captain.

Meantime, the voyage progresses, and with it the Dauber's destiny;

> They lost the Trades soon after; then came calm,
> Light little gusts and rain, which soon increased
> To glorious northers shouting out a psalm
> At seeing the bright blue water silver fleeced;
> Hornwards she rushed, trampling the seas to yeast.

The ship is becoming more difficult to handle. With every justification one of the Dauber's mates enquires,

> '. . . what good can painting do
> Up on a lower topsail stiff with ice,
> With all your little fish-hooks frozen blue?
> Painting won't help you at the weather clew,
> Nor pass your gaskets for you, nor make sail. . . .'

As in *The Everlasting Mercy*, the narrative is interrupted by a passage which must be regretted. This, it is true, serves to give an account of Dauber's past life. It is told by him to a young apprentice who turns out (not surprisingly) to have been asleep most of the time. It is not that the early history of Dauber is irrelevant at this point. The trouble with this protracted interpolation is that it is too detailed, tedious, and at times sentimental. And it does not bear that kind of miniature image of the whole which a truly good digression, or story within a story, possesses. We are anxious to get on with the story, to know what is going to happen when the bad weather comes and to learn how Dauber will fare.

There are seven pages of Dauber's past history, accounting for his break with his father, and sister who

> . . . sat at home, that silent two,
> Wearing the fire out and the evening through,
> Silent, defeated, broken, in despair,
> My plate unset, my name gone, and my chair.

125

which lines I quote to show how far below the tone of the whole poem this section of it falls. Dauber's initiation into art, as told here, is difficult to envisage. He had discovered his mother's drawings hidden away in a loft.

> That rotting sketch-book showed me how and where
> I, too, could get away; and then I knew
> That drawing was the work I longed to do.

which is not very convincingly the way in which an artist discovers his vocation.

An excellent scene follows soon after this, where the Mate takes Dauber's brush from him and tries his hand at painting a ship. The eternal inability of the ignorant man to meet on common ground with the man of sensibility comes out in this encounter. The ignorance of the Mate, the sycophancy of the men, are contained in this episode of the Mate painting a lifelike ship:

> 'Look here. Look there. Now watch this ship of mine.'
> He drew her swiftly from a memory stored.
> 'Good, sir,' the Bosun said, 'you do her fine!'
> 'Ay,' said the mate, 'I do so, by the Lord!
> I'll paint a ship with any man aboard.'
> They hung about his sketch like beasts at bait.
> 'There now, I taught him painting,' said the Mate.

As the ship moves into bad weather approaching the Horn, as Dauber's suspense mounts, so does his status as an artist in his own eyes – the foundation, that is, of his self-image – become shaken.

> And still the Dauber strove, though all men mocked,
> To draw the splendour of the passing thing,
> And deep inside his heart a something locked,

> Long pricking in him, now began to sting —
> A fear of the disasters storm might bring;
> His rank as painter would be ended then —
> He would keep watch and watch like other men.

That is, 'his rank' as a painter in the ship's service, and also
his rank in his own eyes as painter of the sea, would be
ended. The long passage given to Dauber's imaginative
anticipation of the horrors to come is wonderfully done. His
dread of height, his fore-knowledge of the extreme danger of
working aloft through a storm, reach exhaustion-point: there
is a limit to human endurance, even of imaginary terrors;
Dauber finds peace at last in a new turn of thought, a
compensation in aesthetic vision:

>   . . . a thought occurred
> Within the painter's brain like a bright bird:
> That this, and so much like it, of man's toil,
> Compassed by naked manhood in strange places,
> Was all heroic, but outside the coil
> Within which modern art gleams or grimaces;
> That if he drew that line of sailors' faces
> Sweating the sail, their passionate play and change,
> It would be new, and wonderful, and strange.
>
>   . . . .
> That that was what his work meant; it would be
> A training in new vision – a revealing
> Of passionate men in battle with the sea,
> High on an unseen stage, shaking and reefing;
> And men through him would understand their feeling,
> Their might, their misery, their tragic power,
> And all by suffering pain a little hour;

One cannot help feeling that John Masefield's own experience is here depicted, for though it is not essential for an
artist always to have seen, tasted, touched and smelt all he
writes about, it is difficult to imagine any writer who had not
rounded Cape Horn describing it as Masefield does in

Dauber. This desire to reveal through art the activities of the ship, this wonder at – almost reverence for – the sailors' work, which Dauber is made to speak of, they are surely the poet's own. Dauber, then, has started merging his identity with the aesthetic contemplation of the ship. The loss of individuality to which he knows he is doomed as the ship nears the dreaded Horn – a time when he will be but one of 'all hands' called night and day on deck – encroaches on him. Such a negation of himself is wonderfully adumbrated where, just prior to the Cape Horn episode, the fog descends. The scene is portrayed through Dauber's eyes. He is set to the foghorn. It is absolutely right that the poet has placed him there. As the principal protagonist of the story, it is at this moment Dauber alone who must face the dreadful merging into the mute nothingness that surrounds the ship. The most impressive symbolic passage in the poem occurs here; Dauber on the poop makes the warning note (like a self-warning) blare forth,

> Listening lest ice should make the note resound.

Here the fates of Dauber and the ship are intertwined. The responsive echo of ice is what he literally dreads for the ship; and he dreads figuratively, too, the inner response of Dauber-the-artist, turning frigid.

> She bayed there like a solitary hound
> Lost in a covert; all the watch she bayed,
> The fog, come closelier down, no answer made.

No answer, that is, from the inanimate forces, fog and ice. An answer does come, but not till Dauber is become one with the ship and the ship one with the elements:

> Denser it grew, until the ship was lost.
> The elemental hid her; she was merged
> In mufflings of dark death, like a man's ghost,
> New to the change of death, yet thither urged.

Note particularly the image of death which prefigures both the menacing fog and the death of Dauber as artist. The ship is now 'like a man's ghost' as is Dauber. And then comes the response which Dauber, at the foghorn, has been awaiting:

> Then from the hidden waters something surged —
> Mournful, despairing, great, greater than speech,
> A noise like one slow wave on a still beach.
>
> Mournful, and then again mournful, and still
> Out of the night that mighty voice arose;
> The Dauber at his foghorn felt the thrill.
> Who rode that desolate sea? What forms were those?
> Mournful, from things defeated, in the throes
> Of memory of some conquered hunting-ground,
> Out of the night of death arose the sound.
>
> 'Whales!' said the Mate. They stayed there all
>   night long
> Answering the horn. . . .

These mournful creatures, mist-enfolded Moby Dicks, are representations of that part of Dauber which is the artist, the individual, the solitary being, now become objectified. For here the poet is writing on two levels at once. The answer Dauber has been expecting comes not from within himself but from outside, from the solitary strange 'defeated' forms, 'in the throes / Of memory of some conquered hunting-ground', replying all night long to him 'out of the night of death'.

> So the night past, but then no morning broke —

Dauber's metamorphosis is complete. Where before he was motivated by the inner certitude of the artist which gave him his *raison d'être*, he is forced now to turn to a new source of confidence. He is a member of the crew and must justify himself by seamanship.

But as a member of the crew he is particularly helpless and

afraid. Unlike his fellows, he needs bravery in order to brave the terrors aloft. It is sheer willpower that keeps him alive when the ship comes to Cape Horn and he climbs aloft with the men.

> Cursing they came; one kicking out behind,
> Kicked Dauber in the mouth, and one below
> Punched at his calves; the futtock-shrouds inclined,
> It was a perilous path for one to go.

The first appalling hours aloft leave Dauber more wretched and terror-stricken, more prone to the bullying and abuse of the men than ever, despite the fact that he has really worked, suffered and got himself drenched and frozen with the rest. When, after a brief sleep in his sopping-wet bunk, Dauber again hears all hands called, and knows that he must once more face the wild freezing weather aloft, it is the climax of his ineffectuality that prompts his words,

> 'Is it cold on deck?' said Dauber. 'Is it cold?'

– a striking line which, in its austere and uncompromising epitome, substantiates the figure of Dauber in his pathetic latter role.

The direction of the narrative shifts now to enlarge upon the Dauber's emergence from this shrinking ineffectuality into a seaman tested and tried. As such, he is successful. It costs him the pain

> Which crowds a century's torment in a span.
> For the next month the ocean taught this man,
> And he, in that month's torment, while she wested,
> Was never warm nor dry, nor full nor rested

and his gain is 'manhood at the testing-place'.

Accepted now, with the rest of the ship, Dauber none the less hankers after his paints again.

But it is to the credit of the poet's dramatic instinct for narrative, as well as his realistic insight, that he does not show the Dauber emerging triumphant from the situation with a foot in both worlds, a sailor-artist or an artist-sailor. For dramatic and realistic purposes the Dauber must either be artist or seaman. There is no reason, on the surface, why the story should not end happily with Dauber being matey with the Bosun and dabbing his canvas simultaneously. But the organic motivation of the story decrees otherwise. When the fog descended to swallow the ship, the ship and the whole universe which the ship comprises swallowed the artist in Dauber. The last we saw of the artist was in the image, fearful and beautiful, of the whales.

It is dramatically correct that Dauber should die. It is artistically successful that he should be killed in ironic circumstances. When the Mate

> . . . eyed his sail
> And said the Horn was going to flick her tail.

there opens that last phase of the Dauber's story which is both unexpected and natural. (I use the term 'natural' in preference to the ambiguous 'inevitable' which is very often employed to describe what is dramatically appropriate in a work of art, and what is boring.) It is unexpected because already the ship has begun to right herself, the men are beginning to smarten her up for her arrival at their destination. Dauber sings as he scrubs the deck, thinking of the end of the voyage.

> To come, after long months, at rosy dawn,
> Into the placid blue of some great bay.
> Treading the quiet water like a fawn
> Ere yet the morning haze was blown away.
> A rose-flushed figure putting by the grey,
> And anchoring there before the city smoke
> Rose, or the church-bells rang, or men awoke.

The second storm, unforeseen by Dauber, bears conse-
quences which nevertheless have previously occurred to
him. In an earlier stage in the voyage, when he had allowed
his imagination to set forth in advance the fury to come, he
had already anticipated how he might one day 'add a bubble
to the clipper's track'. The thing that is natural about the
coming of the second storm in which the Dauber perished, is
its bitter justice. The fact that such justice has no necessary
relationship with the events preceding it, or that it is not the
actual form of justice that always pertains to real life, does
not concern us. The justice is the true consummation of the
story because, Dauber having fulfilled himself in one sense –
for him a superficial one – to the exclusion of the essential
justification of his being, there is now no justification for him
to live. Psychologically this is sound. No man can serve two
masters. The nobility of Dauber's determination to fight
down his natural abhorrence of danger is unquestioned. But
in the process he loses that part of himself which has a
nobility of its own. The role as a man of action cannot last,
even in real life, if it is adopted by an essentially reflective
being, for he will be half a person.

Some suggestion of Dauber's already divided personality
is given in the final tragic scene. Dauber, working aloft, slips
and falls. But he is not immediately aware of falling; he
thinks it is someone else:

> And there his mate was falling; quick he clutched
> An arm in oilskins swiftly snatched away.
> A voice said 'Christ!' a quick shape stooped and touched,
> Chain struck his hands, ropes shot, the sky was smutched
> With vast black fires that ran, that fell, that furled,
> And then he saw the mast, the small snow hurled.
>
> . . . .
>
> 'I thought it was Tom who fell,' his brain's voice said.

And Tom, the seaman, the true man of action, tells how
Dauber, in falling

. . . clutched at me and almost had me pipped.
He caught my 'ris'band, but the oilskin ripped . . .
It tore clean off. Look here. I was near gone . . .'

meaning, in the inner and figurative sense of the poem, that
Dauber, at heart, desired the destruction of the man-of-
action within himself.

Dauber is the only one of Masefield's poems which I think
lends itself to symbolic probing. It is remarkably outside the
type of work we expect from him, for his main talent is in
broad and various surface depiction. But here he confines
himself to the individual to a far greater degree than
anywhere else; he goes deep. The dramatic value of the poem
is focused in the character of Dauber himself.

III
The Poetry of 'Dauber'

Dauber was published within two years of *The Everlasting
Mercy*. Any doubts as to Masefield's staying-power as a
narrative poet, which arose over his *Widow in the Bye Street*
were dispersed by *Dauber*. Like *The Everlasting Mercy*, it is a
story which, by the intensity of the conception, could not
have been told in prose. *Dauber* contains finer poetry than in
any of the poet's earlier work, and his advance in the poetic
use of language is to be noted.

It is not without relevance that in 1911 Masefield had
written his study of Shakespeare for the Home University
Library. When one speaks of the influence of Shakespeare on
a writer, one is apt to be understood as meaning that a
'Shakespearian' style – perhaps an Elizabethan turn of
phrasing or rhythmic majesty – has emerged. I think
Masefield was influenced by his special studies of Shakespeare, but I mean by this that he was influenced, in so far as
Shakespeare opens the eyes and the ears. It is a common-

133

place of didactic criticism today that poets should not try to write like Shakespeare. The importance to the poet of reading Shakespeare over and over again is insufficiently stressed.

All Masefield's previous experience of Shakespeare was brought to bear on this close study of his work in 1911. I am not dissuaded by the fact that the *Widow in the Bye Street* (1912) shows no exceptional awakening of the senses, from believing that the poet brought to *Dauber* the advantage of his concentrated studies. Such a process as that which occurs between Shakespeare and his serious reader may make an immediate impact on the mind, but may yet lie latent perhaps for some years before the reader, if he is a poet, can give them expression in his own voice.

The poetry of *Dauber* reveals that the poet has, by some means or other, attained a new, more intense awareness of reality. His imagination functions more powerfully, his diction is more original, more compact, his descriptive passages are more firm and clear, than in anything he had formerly written. That is not to say that there is, in *Dauber*, a sustained level of elevated language. This would defeat the purpose of narrative verse which is always pitched on a more intimate, casual note than, say, the ode or the lyric; but there are other reasons why 'high' poetry is scarce in *Dauber*. One reason is that much of the work is done in dialogue. This itself is written and disposed with that great skill which we are entitled to call poetry.

Secondly, there is in *Dauber*, as elsewhere, the characteristic lame page or two here and there which does not simply represent a bridge of monotonous sameness between one exceptional section and another, but which is positively bad verse, really unconsciously comical. Such passages can neither cancel the obvious value of the whole poem nor be removed, but remain there forever with neither good verse nor sound sentiment to redeem them, like a horse-hair shirt to one reader at least.

It would be unprofitable to examine closely such an unfortunate section of the poem as that containing the account of Dauber's home life. But one curious fact is discernible. Whereas at first the fault seems to lie in an acutely sentimental attitude, it soon becomes apparent that the situation itself is not so much in question as the manner in which it is expressed. Which brings us to the realization that an outworn rhyme, a banal phrase, a careless line of dialogue, can alone make a piece of verse sentimental; and conversely that any sentiment, however banal, gains the vitality of a new meaning from the way in which it is expressed. How many of our great poets come to the very verge of sentimentality, but never fall into the abyss? There is nothing intrinsically unacceptable about the Dauber's home-life; the trouble is that it is presented as a conglomerate cliché.

Just as *The Everlasting Mercy* as an entity triumphs over the section devoted to little Jimmy's mother's speech, so does *Dauber* as a whole survive the piece about Dauber's father's heart-break. Both are inspired works. *Dauber* is the better written. The verse-form is peculiarly suited to the subject and is admirably handled. It is a seven-line stanza, with a five-stress line: rhymes: a, b, a, b, b, c, c – Chaucer's *Troilus and Criseyde* form, which is so calm, so relentless, so suitable to the idea of Fate. The most noticeably exalted language in *Dauber* occurs in the verses descriptive of the sea. This is, I think, related to John Masefield's attitude, as a poet, to the sea.

As a poet of the sea, Masefield has an important place in English literature. He is one of the very few poets who write of the sea as from the vantage-point of the ship and not as from the shore. Indeed, it is remarkable how much 'shore' poetry of the sea, compared with 'ship' poetry, has come from sea-faring England. There are of course the poems about naval battles (beloved of the eighteenth century), but they are understandably concerned with the battle and not with the sea. It may be worth noting that earlier poetry gives the closest attention to the sea as a subject from the seafarer's view. The great Anglo-Saxon *Seafarer* itself is vividly, minutely detailed. Even Donne's *The Storme* is by no means a landlocked poem. But soon the seventeenth-century poet William Browne was to write:

> As carefull Merchants doe expecting stand
> (After long time and many gales of wynde)
> Upon the place where the brave ship must land:
> So waite I for the vessell of my mind.

'The vessell of my mind'! – thus foreshadowing that vessel of the soul which bore the Ancient Mariner. The Romantics wrote much about the sea – always as an image, not as a subject; never as a real, workable tangible element – and nearly always seen from the shore: look at any of Swinburne's many sea poems. And Darley, writing of the sea in *Nepenthe*, drowns his 'poor youth' in a substance which is hardly salt water but some sulphurous liquid from the cavernous recesses of the heart. In depicting the real sea, and not just an impression of it, the Romantics were at sea in Edward Lear's sieve.

But in the eighteenth century, William Falconer who, like Masefield, was an experienced seafarer, wrote a long epic of a real voyage which is distinguished from much sea-verse of the time in that Neptune and the Nymphs are not dragged in on every other page. *The Shipwreck* (1762) has nothing like the flexibility, the depth, of *Dauber*, but it has this in common with the later poem, that it is about real sea-life. Falconer, like the later poet, was not afraid to put the technical language of ships into verse:

> The yards again ascend each comrade mast,
> The leeches taut, the halyards are made fast,
> The bow-lines hauled, and yards to starboard braced,
> And straggling ropes in pendent order placed.

The main-sail, by the squall so lately rent,
In streaming pendants flying, is unbent:
With brails refixed, another soon prepared,
Ascending, spreads along beneath the yard.
To each yard-arm the head-rope they extend,
And soon their earings and their robans bend.
That task performed, they first braces slack,
Then to the chesstree drag the unwilling tack.
And, while the lee clue-garnet's lowered away,
Taut aft the sheet they tally, and belay.

(*The Shipwreck. Canto II.*)

This is the sort of thing Masefield often does, being, like
Falconer, fond of naming the parts of a ship and going into
the details of how things are done. So, in *Dauber*, part of the
poetry lies in these simple evocative words which stand for
objects unfamiliar to most people, yet altogether real. For
example,

They reached the crojick yard, which buckled, buckled
Like a thin whalebone to the topsail's strain.
They laid upon the yard and heaved and knuckled,
Pounding the sail, which jangled and leapt again.

And here, this sense of things being done in the proper way:

They stowed the sail, frapping it round with rope,
Leaving no surface for the wind, no fold,

But added to the poetic value of these fascinating names of
parts and their functions, there is a greater enrichment in the
use of metaphor and simile. Note in the last passage but one
quoted above, the image 'thin whalebone' to account for the
bending yard – an image which, at the time when whalebone
was still in much use, may have had a more immediate
impact on the reader than it does now, but which, in losing
its topicality, seems to have gained a deeper quality; it
becomes more important. Where the image of whalebone

may have suggested women's stays to the reader of 1913 (and still, of course, it was a successful image, meaning exactly what the poet meant), today the image calls forth the two ideas 'whale' and 'bone' – suggesting that solitude and naked hardness which is so in keeping with the whole poem. This, I do not think the poet envisaged. Good poetry and, particularly, good imagery is like that. The poet means and says one thing to his generation, and if what he says is durable it will mean something else, to another generation but not always what the poet meant. The descriptive passages in particular are alive with original imagery, and close-packed diction.

> Darker it grew, still darker, and the stars
> Burned golden, and the fiery fishes came.
> The wire-note loudened from the straining spars;
> The sheet-blocks clacked together always the same,
> The rushing fishes streaked the seas with flame,
> Racing the one speed noble as their own:
> What unknown joy was in those fish unknown!

Whether it is that these phenomena are to be taken as observed through the Dauber's enamoured eyes, or whether because the poet has felt instinctively that an intensified piece of observation should follow upon the flatter passages of dialogue that precede it, these highly-coloured rapid word-paintings are very effective, placed exactly where they are. Beside the crude shouting of the men, the common business of the ship, and the various plain humdrum activities, the outer world of nature is given a sudden exaggerated fame. The poet has planted in their midst stars which 'burn golden'; the fishes are 'fiery' and 'rushing', they 'streaked the seas with flame'. Note the unusual participle 'loudened' – there are many such examples in *Dauber* of near-neologisms – and the slight but effective alteration in rhythm in line four.

These descriptions are seldom alike in kind. There is the impressionism of

> Names in the darkness passed and voices cried;
> The red spark glowed and died, the faces seemed
> As things remembered when a brain has died,
> To all but high intenseness deeply dreamed.
> Like hissing spears the fishes' fire streamed,
> And on the clipper rushed with tossing mast,
> A bath of flame broke round her as she passed.

– its economical suggestiveness; and there is the vivid poster-paint realism of

> A naked seaman washing a red shirt
> Sat at a tub whistling between his teeth;
> Complaining blocks quavered like something hurt,
> A sailor cut an old boot for a sheath,
> The ship bowed to her shadow-ship beneath,
> And little slaps of spray came at the roll
> On to the deck-planks from the scupper-hole.

– where the scene is outlined in sharp details of sight and sound – the colour of the seaman's shirt, the noise of the blocks, the 'shadow-ship' to which the heaving ship 'bows', and the 'slaps of spray'.

And these graphic sections of the narrative are distinguished from the more lax and level parts which deal with action and speech, by the introduction of startling fragments of imagery and words used in an original way. These leaven the descriptive passages. The poet speaks of 'the proud ship's pawings', making the ship into a mighty beast; later he describes the ship as 'Proud, with taut bridles, pawing . . .' The sky above the sea is 'dusty with moonlight' – endowing the banal poetic moonlight with the quality of lit-up dust. The sleeping men are 'bunched like the dead'. The ship, once more a beast, drinks 'great draughts of roller at her hawse'. Snow falling at night is 'an aimless dust out of a confused heaven'; while the snow-storms of Cape Horn are depicted as

> . . . heavens that fell and never ceased to fall,
> And ran in smoky snatches along the sea,

Through the snow is seen 'the eyeless sun plucked out and going' – a curious telescoped figure – we imagine the eyes of the sun being plucked out, though it is stated that the sun itself is 'plucked'; and so we have both meanings.

When the sky darkens over at the beginning of the great storm, the abstract, amorphous thing, darkness itself, is given the outlines of an enormous creature with devouring jaws and crushing hooves, in the line 'The blackness crunched all memory of the sun'. In fact the whole image is brought before us through the one word *crunched*. And in the well-known description of the rounding of Cape Horn, the image of the ship as an animal takes definite shape:

> The ship lay – the sea smote her, the wind's bawl
> Came, 'loo, loo, loo!' The devil cried his hounds
> On to the poor spent stag strayed in his bounds.

Thus the poet, a lover of the sights and sounds of hunting, discovers in the wind's 'loo, loo, loo!' an echo of the hunting cries of the countryside, and transforms the wind into a demon-hunter, the ship to a 'spent stag'.

Later in the poem the ship

> . . . was hounded
> North, while the wind came; like a stag she ran
> Over grey hills and hollows of seas wan.
> She had a white bone in her mouth:[1] she sped;

[1] In response to an enquiry about this phrase, Masefield wrote to the author, 'The phrase, "carrying a bone in her mouth", used often to be applied to sailing-vessels that had a fair wind and had a wash of white water across their bows. The ship often looked like a creature advancing carrying a big white bone.'

The last action of Dauber, furling the sails just before he falls, is conveyed in an ominous simile where a wilder beast is suggested:

> The three sails leaped together, yanking high,
> Like talons darting up to clutch the sky.

This type of language is not sustained, nor is it meant to be so. It gains edge from the dialogue as the dialogue is enhanced by the descriptive parts. On a level midway between the two are the plain narrative lines which are not always as good as they could be.

The reported speech of *Dauber*, is, however, the best thing Masefield has done in dialogue. It has more ease than the spoken word in the poet's previous work, and in none of his subsequent poems has he allowed himself the rhythmic scope that we find in *Dauber*. We find lines like this, a shuttlecock type of dialogue, full of movement:

> 'Please, sir, they spoiled my drawings.' 'Who did?'
>   'They.'
> 'Who's they?' 'I don't quite know, sir.'
> 'Don't quite know, sir?
> Then why are you aft to talk about it, hey?
> Whom d'you complain of?' 'No one.' 'No one?' 'No,
>   sir.'
> 'Well, then, go forward till you've found them. Go, sir.
> If you complain of someone, then I'll see.
> Now get to hell! and don't come bothering me.'

There is also the composite dialogue-picture which is a feature of more recent poetry and fiction – fragments of speech fused into a whole.

> 'Caught in her ball-dress,' said the Bosun, hauling;
> 'Lee-ay, lee-ay' quick, high, came the men's call;
> It was all wallop of sails and startled calling.

'Let fly!' 'Let go!' 'Clew up!' and 'Let go all!'
'Now up and make them fast!' 'Here, give us a haul!'
'Now up and stow them! Quick! By God! we're done!'

Or, on occasion, the speech may be casual, conversational and loose, usually marked with that peculiar sardonic spleen of the sailors' jargon:

He flung the door half open, and a sea
Washed them both in, over the splashboard, down
'You silly, salt miscarriage!' sputtered he.
'Dauber, pull out the plug before we drown!
That's spoiled my laces and my velvet gown.
Where is the plug?' Groping in pitch dark water,
He sang between his teeth 'The Farmer's Daughter'.

Or else it might be a phrase which serves to intensify our consciousness of Dauber's plight:

Them's rotten sea-boots, Dauber, that you brought.

And, when those men who had done their best to crush the artist gather round the dying Dauber, their simple, slack, articulations come like a mockery:

'Ask if he's got a message. Hell, he's gone!
Here, Dauber, paints. . . .'

I said that the plain narrative passages were not always successful. Those which bring the poem to an end, however, seem to me the high peak of the poetry of *Dauber*. Here, the narrative proper blends almost unnoticeably with the speech. The lines are natural and moving and restrained.

Night fell, and all night long the Dauber lay
Covered upon the table; all night long
The pitiless storm exulted at her prey,

Huddling the waters with her icy thong.
But to the covered shape she did no wrong.
He lay beneath the sailcloth. Bell by bell
The night wore through; the stars rose, the stars fell.

. . . .

He was off duty. So it blew all night,
And when the watches changed the men would come
Dripping within the door to strike a light
And stare upon the Dauber lying dumb,
And say, 'He come a cruel thump, poor chum.'
Or, 'He'd a-been a fine big man'; or, 'He . . .
A smart young seaman he was getting to be.'

Or, 'Damn it all, it's what we've all to face!'. . .

In that justly celebrated stanza which describes the ship
moving into fair weather after Dauber's burial, the tone is
fluent and peaceful; the catharsis achieved, 'all passion
spent'.

Then in the sunset's flush they went aloft,
And unbent sails in the most lovely hour
When the light gentles and the wind is soft,
And beauty in the heart breaks like a flower.
Working aloft they saw the mountain tower,
Snow to the peak; they heard the launchmen shout;
And bright along the bay the lights came out.

Seven

'Reynard the Fox'

I
Definitions

Because, to me, *Reynard the Fox* is so satisfying and leaves so little to be desired, I begin with the question, what kind of a poem is it? About the early poems, since they express the poet as yet unformed, it seems necessary to seek the influence of other poets upon them – to discover how the poet himself was using this traditional inheritance, what he was adding that was new, from himself. With *The Everlasting Mercy*, the test was one of psychological penetration; in *Dauber*, I have felt that the thing to look for is a constructive sense, involving the symbolic structure in its relation to the structure of the verse. But since *Reynard the Fox* has a quality which seems like completeness; since, in John Squire's words, the poet 'has pulled off with *Reynard*', I am prompted to define first and analyse afterwards; what kind of poem is it? And the first answer that occurs to me is that it is a classic narrative of events. I mean 'classic' in the sense that it is a finished, consummate, work of its kind; and I use 'narrative of events' to mean that the important thing about the story is the balanced sequence of events. The opening is no less important than the outcome; the characters are no more important than the location; the verse is no less important than the conception of the poem. This is a work about which one cannot easily say that the author was 'trying to do'

144

something as we might say that in *Prometheus Unbound* Shelley was trying to express a humanist ideal, or that in *The Temple* George Herbert was attempting to stabilize the relationship between the people and the Church, the Church and God.

That is where I think Middleton Murry went wrong about *Reynard the Fox*. Murry wrote one of the few essays that one could respect on John Masefield. Essays on Masefield tended to be either adulatory or vituperative, and Murry's is more sober. 'Mr. Masefield,' he writes, 'is gradually finding his way to his self-appointed end, which is the glorification of England in narrative verse. . . . We feel that he now approaches what he desires to do with some certainty of doing it.'[1]

His *self-appointed end . . . what he desires to do* – It is strange, how many critics imagine that a poet starts out from a known point to traverse a charted course in order to arrive at a precognized end.

Murry was, of course, partly right. Masefield did set out to do something and 'the glorification of England' is one of the things *Reynard the Fox* carries with it. But when it comes to the point, this talk about 'the glorification of England' is merely a critic's abstraction. What the poet was attempting was not a fulfilment of an abstract theory but the recording, in verse, of a fox-hunt. The difference is important, because if you are looking in the poem for an achievement which can be summed up as 'the glorification of England' you will miss a lot, and you are not likely to find much more than Murry found. But if you are looking for a fox-hunt in verse, you will get it.

What Murry found was determined by what he was seeking. Instead of the glorification of England he found nostalgia – 'We seem to detect,' he wrote, 'behind his superfluity of technical, and at times archaic phrase, an

[1]The Nostalgia of Mr. Masefield (*Aspects of Literature*, 1920).

unconscious desire to convince himself that he is saturated in essential Englishness, and we incline to think that even his choice of subject was less inevitable than self-imposed.'

But, why should a subject not be self-imposed? It is a pleasant fancy that a poet simply waits, watches and listens until something 'inevitable' turns up. But in reality, a poet may wait, watch and listen without success for ever unless he imposes a subject on himself. And to cap his claim for John Masefield's nostalgia, Murry chose to compare a passage from *Reynard* with a passage from Chaucer. In so doing, the critic succeeded in demonstrating something other than what he intended. Though he does not, as he claimed, show a difference in the tone of the poets, his juxtaposition of the two passages simply reveals that Chaucer was the better hand at verse. But he insists that we note Chaucer's naturalness as against Masefield's nostalgia, forgetting that Chaucer, too, had his nostalgia. And nostalgia is not necessarily out of place in poetry.

This censure was written in 1920, at a time when, in the critic's own words, 'the desperate *bergerie* of the Georgian era' was rife. An overstrained effort to 'capture' the countryside of England, which he thought he detected in *Reynard*, is certainly present in most Georgian poetry. Perhaps the critic was looking too hard for this particular flaw and was too much expecting to find it. Reading the poem today, there seems very little of the Georgian in it; the archaisms have clicked into place; the England which Masefield portrayed is all but past, but the poem raises no doubts that it existed. What does strike the reader today, however, is that the poem is the work of a poet in sympathy with Chaucer, and this cannot be said of Murry who, in the same essay, claims that 'Chaucer is hardly what we understand as a great poet'.

Reynard the Fox is a classic of its kind; a panoramic record of an English rural community seen rather in the manner in which the painter Frith saw Derby Day and other gregarious aspects of his country. Masefield's view, like Frith's, is an approving one, the approval takes the existence of an object as its justification.

There is, in fact, no 'moral' to the story of *Reynard*. The Hunt meets and pursues the fox. The fox gets away; however, another fox is caught – an anonymous fox with whose fate the reader has not previously been involved. Hence, the fox which gets caught has no reality outside that one fact, that it is caught; it is a fact the absence of which would leave the poem without its full catharsis, it would frustrate the purpose of the meet and render fruitless the careful delineation of each member. But Reynard the Fox who gets away – it is eminently just that he should escape. For should Reynard have been caught and killed after so many escapes, this would likewise impair the catharsis.

The poem is not a tract against fox-hunting, nor a piece of propaganda for fox-hunting. The tone of the work compares favourably with the self-defeating sentimental animal poetry of such writers as Ralph Hodgson. The high degree of objectivity in *Reynard*, accompanied yet with so much vitality and suspense (so that the 'objectivity' is not such that the poem seems hardly to have been worth the poet's effort), is what I personally find so attractive.

The type of art rarely succeeds in which moral judgment is suspended; it is rarely desirable; in times like our own it is impossible to practise. But where it has succeeded in the past, I think it will attract readers in times like our own, by its very saneness and solidity in which moral values are implicit.

Such art is largely self-explanatory. It needs neither the critic-hierophant nor the critic-philosopher to explain or expound it. The most I can therefore endeavour to do is to locate some of the technical achievements of the present work.

But before going on to do so, I would like to point out that, although there is no 'moral' to the narrative, the *moral vision*

147

of the poet, which appears in all his stories, is not lacking here. This moral vision may be described as a profound sense and love of uniqueness in all the visible world.

II
The Plan of the Poem

For those who are about to read *Reynard the Fox* for the first time, the best approach is possibly to read the poem first, then Masefield's essay on fox-hunting, and then the poem again.

The essay *Fox-Hunting*, which was printed in America as a preface to the poem, is also to be found in the poet's collection *Recent Prose* (1926). It is so much a part of the poem that the two should, perhaps, always be printed together; the prose is, moreover, so well written that it could not but adorn a book.

In this essay the poet writes, 'At a fox-hunt, and nowhere else in England, except perhaps at a funeral, can you see the whole of the land's society brought together, focused for the observer, as the Canterbury Pilgrims were for Chaucer.'

'This fact,' he continues, 'made the subject attractive. The fox-hunt gave an opportunity for a picture or pictures of the members of the English community.' (The subject, you will note, with reference to Middleton Murry's claim, is a *fox-hunt*, not 'the glorification of England'. And the '*picture* of the members of the English community' which the subject was chosen to provide is not the same thing as glorification.)

What the Canterbury Pilgrims were for Chaucer, so is the meet for John Masefield. 'I have at all times endeavoured to look steadily at my subject,' said Wordsworth. Like Chaucer, and unlike Wordsworth, Masefield at all times does look steadily at his subject.

What he learned from Chaucer, in fact, was how to look at his subject steadily enough not to get the vision blurred.

Thus, he has in his mind the exact appearance, character-istics, and name of everyone partaking in the Hunt. He knows every ditch and field of Ghost Heath Run by heart. He knows the horses and the hounds, each one; and he knows the fox. They are all imaginary and he knows them all.

'Some have asked,' he writes, 'whether the Ghost Heath Run is founded on any recorded run of any real Hunt. It is not. It is an imaginary run, in country made up of many different pieces of country, some of them real, some of them imaginary.

'These real and imaginary fields, woods and brooks are taken, as they exist, from Berkshire, where the fox lives, from Herefordshire, where he was found, from Trapalanda, Gloucestershire, Buckinghamshire, Herefordshire, Wor-cestershire and Berkshire, where he ran, from Trapalanda where he nearly died, and from a wild and beautiful corner in Berkshire where he rests from his run.'

Not only the Run but the people, horses, hounds and fox are composite creations. Once created, the poet has his eye steadily upon them. He discerns not only the appearance of them but the smells and sounds of the hunt, arriving early at 'The Cock and Pye':

> To fill that quiet width of road
> As full of men as Framilode
> Is full of sea when tide is in.

He perceives the separate activities, sights, sounds and smells, insignificant in themselves but which, taken to-gether, signify the beginning of the story:

> A pad-groom gave a cloth a beating,
> Knocking the dust out with a stake.
> Two men cleaned stalls with fork and rake,
> And one went whistling to the pump,
> The handle whined, ker-lump, ker-lump,
> The water splashed into the pail,

And, as he went, it left a trail,
Lipped over on the yard's bricked paving.
Two grooms (sent on before) were shaving
There in the yard, at glasses propped
On jutting bricks; they scraped and stropped,
And felt their chins and leaned and peered.

This is very steady and close observation. The apparently random selection of trivia is in reality very deliberate. Small sensations are evoked, scraps of conversation recorded, to create the general feeling of something about to begin:

Blue smoke from strong tobacco drifted
Out of the yard, the passers snifft it,
Mixed with the strong ammonia flavour
Of horses' stables and the savour
Of saddle-paste and polish spirit
Which put the gleam on flap and tirrit.
The grooms in shirts with rolled-up sleeves,
Belted by girths of coloured weaves,
Groomed the clipped hunters in their stalls.
One said: 'My dad cured saddle-galls,
He called it Dr. Barton's cure –
Hog's lard and borax, laid on pure.'
And others said: 'Ge' back, my son.'
'Stand over, girl; now, girl, ha' done.'
'Now, boy, no snapping; gently. Crikes!
He gives a rare pinch when he likes.'

The people who ride up one by one to the 'Cock and Pye', or arrive on foot, on cycles or in dog-carts, are as miscellaneous a collection of living people, depicted to the life, as Elizabethan drama produced. And whereas, for instance, the characters of Dickens are in a world of their own: 'Dickensia', these people are gathered together outside the 'Cock and Pye' in a perfectly normal world.

Now two things are worth noting about this collection of people. First they are not just man-in-the-mass. That sense of uniqueness I have mentioned as characteristic of the poet is a salient feature in *Reynard*. Each character is different from the others. Secondly, it should be observed that the points of difference between characters are reconciled by their common purpose, and what would otherwise become a scattered sequence becomes a pageant. Now the poet has faith in this pageant, he really observes every part of it. His belief in its reality finds an immediate response in the reader.

And these people are depicted, each within a very few lines. In a novel, the characters may not emerge in their entirety until the last chapter; in a play, likewise. But in a poem like *Reynard*, the people who are introduced are not there for the purpose of working out their individual destinies. They cannot develop. No one's nature and status is in any way altered by the fox-hunt. Therefore, all that we are to know of them, individually, has to be presented within a few compact lines. We are not of course to know a great deal about them. We do not expect maturity and depth from the figures in a pageant; what is needed is that each should be distinct and special and able to perform with verisimilitude.

This is, in fact, just what the people in *Reynard* do; for their function they are admirable, existing each without much personal history; and with a lack of personal perspective almost mediaeval in concept.

Within the self-imposed limits of this thumb-nail pictorial method Masefield depicts his characters in various ways, supplementing a descriptive statement with a list of carefully-chosen things which the person in question does or does not do.

Thus, the parson

> . . . did not talk of churchyard worms
> But of our privilege as dust

We learn that

> He loved the sound of his own voice,

that he was

> Well-knit, well-made, well-coloured, eager.
> He kept no Lent to make him meagre,
> He loved his God, himself and man,
> He never said, 'Life's wretched span;
> This wicked world,' in any sermon.

and that

> Some grey cathedral in a town
> Where drowsy bells toll out the time
> To shaven closes sweet with lime . . .
> Was certain some day to be his
> Nor would a mitre go amiss
> To him, because he governed well.
> His voice was like the tenor bell
> When services were said and sung,
> And he had read in many a tongue,
> Arabic, Hebrew, Spanish, Greek.

We get to know these people, also, by what they look like and by what they say or is said to them; and the poet sometimes makes a scrap of dialogue serve the purpose of description; sometimes an anecdote, told by a third party, gives us our information.

The poet introduces the idea of a community, with common memories stretching back into the past, by such methods as in the following piece (reminiscent of Thomas Hardy though it is) on Pete Gurney, a dairy farmer:

> One grief he had, a grief still new,
> That former Parson joined with Squire
> In putting down the Playing Quire
> In church, and putting organ in.

'Ah, boys, that was a pious din,
That Quire was; a pious praise
The noise was that we used to raise,
I and my serpent, George with his'n,
On Easter Day, in "He is risen",
Or blessed Christmas in "Venite".
And how the trombone came in mighty
In Alleluias from the heart!
Pious, for each man played his part,
Not like 'tis now.' Thus he, still sore
For changes forty years before.

And the period of the poem – the early years of this century –
are delightfully suggested in a few lines:

Two bright young women, nothing meek,
Rode up on bicycles and propped
Their wheels in such wise that they dropped
To bring the parson's son to aid.
Their cycling suits were tailor-made.

One of the most satisfactory things about the poem is its
precision. Everything is named – people, hounds and horses;
every field, hill and wood through which Reynard is pursued
has a name. This naming of things serves two successful
purposes – it gives a plausible aspect to the Hunt and to the
geographical location of Ghost Heath Run, and it gives edge
to the verbal texture of the poem.

Consider the names of horses: Stormalong (by Tempest
out of Love-me-Long) and Chinese-White (from Lilybud by
Mandarin) and of hounds: Joyful, Arrogant, Catch-him,
Damsel, Skylark, Tarrybreeks, Daffodil; and of places:
Tencombe Regis, Slaughter's Court, Nun's Wood Yews,
Hungry Hill, Seven Springs Mead, Deerlip Brook, Ghost
Heath Wood, Uppat's Leas. They are not quite real, but
they are almost real, which is just what is required for a
story. They come into the verse very nicely, too; they are
lyrical.

The most important thing about *Renard* is the movement. There is the meet, and then there is the Hunt with suspense always sustained and with the verse kept on a swift, exciting tempo; and then there is final satisfaction against all the odds. And though the narrative moves so rapidly, there is a plethora of minute detail, a wealth of imagery and figurative language.

> The rise, which shut the field away,
> Showed him the vales' great map spread out,
> The down's lean flank and thrusting snout,

and:

> Each horse was trembling as a spear
> Trembles in hand when tense to hurl.
> They saw the brimmed brook's eddies curl;
> The willow-roots like Water-snakes;

and:

> The loitering water, flooded full,
> Had yeast on its lip like raddled wool,
> It was wrinkled over with Arab script
> Of eddies that twisted up and slipt.

Reynard himself is seen purely as a creature of instinct:

> He felt that the unseen link which bound
> His spine to the nose of the leading hound
> Was snapped. . . .

expresses the fox's sense that the hounds are off his scent; and his final terrific effort is shown as one complete sense-impression of noises and objects intermingled. Reynard runs

> Till the wood behind seemed risen from root,
> Crying and crashing, to give pursuit,
> Till the trees seemed hounds and the air seemed
>   cry.

There are some interesting and successful experiments with pure description – experiments which seem analagous to film technique. At one moment we have a close-up of a rider:

> He faced the fence and put her through it,
> Shielding his eyes lest spikes should blind him:
> The crashing blackthorn closed behind him.
> Mud-scatters chased him as he scudded;
> His mare's ears cocked, her neat feet thudded.

and in the next verse, comes the relative, bird's-eye-glimpse:

> The kestrel cruising over meadow
> Watched the hunt gallop on his shadow,
> Wee figures, almost at a stand,
> Crossing the multicoloured land,
> Slow as a shadow on a dial.

And this change of focus also has the effect of forcing the reader to slow down the pace of reading, without there having been any metrical change.

The great distinction of *Reynard the Fox* is that it achieves what the poet intended it to do: to record the excitement, the colour and splendour, the sense-impressions and emotions brought into being by a fox-hunt – and not only a representative, a symbolic or 'poetic' hunt but a likely (though imaginary) hunt that took place across Ghost Heath Run, beginning at dawn, at

> . . . 'The Cock and Pye
> By Charles and Martha Enderby,'

and ending when

John Masefield

The beech-wood grey rose dim in the night
With moonlight fallen in pools of light,
The long dead leaves on the ground were rimed;
A clock struck twelve and the church-bells chimed.

Eight

The Narrative Prose

Since *Reynard the Fox*, Masefield's highest achievements in narrative writing have been in prose. Up to the years of the First World War, his prose presents a case parallel to that of his early verse, in the sense that it possesses some intrinsic value and that it was preparation for the mature work, his later novels. And, unlike the poems, the early prose reveals the influence of Irish writers, George Moore and others. It has something, here and there, of the *Maladie du Siècle*, the twinge, the nostalgia, the regret: all transparently an assumed attitude in John Masefield's case, but something, it appears, that had to be undergone. There is also, as in *Salt Water Ballads*, a good deal of the practical seaman, which on the whole Masefield succeeded surprisingly well in combining with the aura of roses, wine and decline.

But right from the start, no matter the lack of consistency, he was a first-rate story-teller. I suppose he began by owing a lot to that other practising seaman and born story-teller, Joseph Conrad, and if so, he presently moved quite away from Conrad's influence.

For one thing, Masefield lacks the tremendousness of Conrad's ability to call up furious emotional undercurrents. And Masefield is less of the word-artist. On the other hand, he never strains after fundamentals which, in Conrad as often as not, turn up in a brewed-up form like the storm-pieces inserted for, but without, effect. Conrad is always consciously the artist; his sailors feel what Conrad himself felt (for otherwise where does the crew of Conrad's *Narcissus*, for example, get its excruciating subtlety from?). Masefield never touches up his characters in this way, though he rarely reaches Conrad's access of understanding. Masefield is more the objective, Conrad more the subjective, artist.

In a fascinating early work by Masefield, *On the Spanish Main* (1906), there is evidence not quite of an affinity with Conrad, but of a temporary discipleship. This is discernible for the most part in the prose style, and it is an exotic quality which Masefield courageously relinquished for the more austere and temperate manner that he made his own from about 1927.

On the Spanish Main is not fiction, of course. It is a factual history, done in the story-telling genre (but not as 'historical' fiction), of the looting expeditions of Drake and other sixteenth-century buccaneers in the West Indies. This served as an introduction to Masefield's sea stories, and some of the historical events he recounts are to be found incorporated in his novels. Drake's attack on Nombre Dios, for example, reappears with slight alterations in the novel *Captain Margaret*. Here is the account from the history – surely one of the most graphic of modern historical works:

> The drum beat up gallantly, the trumpets blew points of war, and the poor citizens, scared from their beds, and not yet sure of their enemy, stood shivering in the dawn, 'marvelling what the matter might be'. In a few moments the two companies were entering the Plaza, making a dreadful racket as they marched, to add to the confusion of the townsfolk, who thought them far stronger than they really were. . . . The church bell was still ringing when Drake's party stormed into the square from the road leading to the sea.

There is much else in this work to anticipate the novels.

There is action, excitement, effort, glorious success and glorious failure. There is colour and profusion, reminiscent of *Salt Water Ballads* ('All in the feathered palm-tree tops the bright green parrots screech. . . .'):

> The channels twisted sluggishly among a multitude of islands, which were gorgeous with rhododendron shrubs, and alive with butterflies, blue and scarlet, that sunned themselves, in blots of colour upon the heavy green leaves. Among the blossomed branches there were parrots screaming and the little humming-birds, like flying jewels darting from flower to flower.

Masefield has placed the year 1911 as the year in which he really began to write. It certainly was the year of his success – the year when, with *The Everlasting Mercy*, he became an established writer. But to ignore (as he advises) all that was written before that date would be to obscure many valuable pieces, among them one of his most fascinating books. This is *A Tarpaulin Muster*, first published in 1907, which I have mentioned earlier. It is a collection of stories and prose sketches, some semi-biographical. The remarkable thing about this collection is that it embodies a practical demonstration of John Masefield's stylistic development. There is, in this volume, an embryonic sample of all the various methods of prose-writing he later adopted. This is a work essential for the study of John Masefield, and it is besides a book of many delights. There are not many copies about, but it is worth getting hold of one.

The story *Edward Herries*, with which the book opens, is essentially a 'young man's story' of the period. It begins thus:

> Edward Herries, the poet, rose from his chair, and looked through the window over the darkening valley. The moon had risen over the tree-tops, and the yews made black patches here and there in the mass of trembling branches ridging the hill. He flung back the curtain, so that he might see better; and the

moonlight, falling upon him, made yet more pale the paleness of his refined face, now wrung with sorrow. . . .

Immature and mannered though it is, this is a style John Masefield developed beyond recognition. He tempered it to the needs of sea-fearing narrative with some success. At this stage the author was attempting to clear a way through the jungle of words into which most good writers are tempted.

The second 'story' in the book – a short fragment or reminiscence – has much of this ornate manner, but here the superficial phraseology of the first story is lacking, and we see that what the author has been striving for is symbolist expression, and that where before he had caught merely the expression, without even the symbols, he now has not only the symbols, but what they symbolize. Here, then, is an extract from *A White Night*:

> We got out our oars and shoved off through the haze. The red-haired man took out a cigar and tried to light it, but the head of the match came off and burnt his fingers. He swore curtly. The officer laughed. 'Remember the boat's crew,' he said. In the darkness, amid the gurgle of the running water, over which the haze came stealthily, the words were like words heard in a dream. I repeated them to myself as I rowed, wondering where I had heard them before. It seemed to me that they had been said before, somewhere, very long ago, and that if I could remember where I should know more than any man knew.

But other pieces in this volume are in quite a different mode. There are some lively sea-stories, where the author's flair for plain story-telling is not merely a promise, it is already a mastery. In the following piece observe how rapidly the story gets going, in its easy colloquial idiom, the opening paragraph of which gives some idea of the semi-realistic semi-fantastic theme:

> 'Once upon a time,' said the sailor, 'the Devil and Davy Jones

came to Cardiff, to the place called Tiger Bay. They put up at Tony Adams's, not far from Pier Head, at the corner of Sunday Lane. And all the time they stayed there they used to be going to the rumshop, where they sat at a table, smoking their cigars, and dicing each other for different persons' souls. Now you must know that the Devil gets landsmen, and Davy Jones gets sailor-folk; and they got tired of having always the same, so then they dice each other for some of another sort. . . .'

Others among these short tales are purely realistic – plain reportage, almost; but always revealing the author's knack of gripping the reader's attention. As in *Salt Water Ballads* these prose-pieces are often stories within stories, told by a sailor. One of the chief delights of this small book is a tale called *The Bottom of the Well* which must be one of the first shaggy dog stories, and which I would by no means say more about and thus spoil it for those who have not read it. There are also ghost stories and fairy tales.

A Tarpaulin Muster is more than a period curiosity, though it is that as well. It is one of those attractive oddities which contain unexpected riches. Such a book (it is only 172 small pages) hardly ever appears today; the tales are all very short but they are self-contained separate experiments, of varying value.

Among the novels by John Masefield which appeared before *The Everlasting Mercy*, the outstanding ones are *Captain Margaret* (1908), *Lost Endeavour* (1910) and *Jim Davis* (1911). These three books represent a trial period for the author. He was purifying his style and adapting it to the novel-length narrative; he was attempting to solve problems of character-ization. One thing that seems to have been settled in his mind at an early stage is the sort of themes he was going to devote himself to: he has of course employed a great variety of themes, but the common element in all of them is adventure of one kind or another. He began writing, as he has always written, whether in poetry or prose, about the sort of thing that would go well in a ballad.

The problems of style and characterization are in conflict in *Captain Margaret*. It is a sea story which embodies a love story. The love story is in conflict with the story of the sea. Consequently, it is a very uneven work. The characters are either over-idealized or crude. The writing is partly of that type which may be called 'fine writing', and which is in these days frequently cried down. But there is much hardy action and hard dialogue in *Captain Margaret*. I said the characterization is sometimes crude; so it is, but this very lack of subtlety has the advantage of sharply delineating the issues of the story. The love tale, superimposed on the adventure narrative, centres round a sensuous lout named Stukely, sensitive Captain Margaret and a rather insipid girl. Of Stukely, it is written:

> . . . his body had a kind of large splendour, it was the splendour of the prize cabbage, of the prize pig, a splendour really horrible. It is horrible to see any large thing without intelligence. . . .

and

> . . . this mass of mucous membrane, boorishly informed, lit only by the marsh-lights of indulged sense. . . .

and again,

> He was more rude to women than to men, partly because he feared them less; but partly because his physical tastes were gross, so that he found pleasure in all horse-play – such as the snatching of handkerchiefs and trinkets, or even of kisses – in gaining which he had to touch or maul his victims, whether protesting or acquiescent.

This is realistic enough, though it is the unassimilated realism of an indignant, sensitive and inexperienced observer.

But the tendency to overstress his characters was mastered by the time *Lost Endeavour* appeared, and this, I think, is partly due to the discipline afforded by Masefield's experiments with drama during this interval (when *The Tragedy of Nan*, among other plays, was produced). While, as the poet admits, he does not possess dramatic talent to any great degree, the composition of these plays does seem to have introduced him to the fundamentals of character-ization. He appears aware henceforward of the interplay of contradictions which every character of fiction must be shown to possess (or not to possess, as the case may be, the point being that an inner dialectic is the norm). The simple outline of a character which the reader is, in effect, invited to fill in according to taste, will not do. I do not mean that Masefield anywhere in his work is concerned to examine or analyse the human process of conflict, but only claim that about the time that he started writing plays he also started putting more convincing characters into his novels; and that these characters are more convincing by virtue of their seeming ability to respond to each other; and that the portrayal of this ability gives an effect of malleability of character; it shows that the author is aware of the interaction of forces within the character; he is aware of motives, choices, emotions, which in turn affect the response between different people. Masefield's characters are as a rule indi-cated by their outwardness, and this is different from being indicated only by an outline.

Lost Endeavour therefore, marks an important advance in the author's narrative art. Not only that, it is one of his best novels. He adopts the method of providing alternate narrators. The story itself has a charged quality (something like old-fashioned 'atmosphere' is what I mean); it has something of Thomas Hardy; the theme is similar in some respects to that of a novel called *Faraway* by J.B. Priestley – the latter book by no means as real, as well-told or as moving as *Lost Endeavour*. This novel has feeling of a deeper order than is to be found in much of Masefield's later, more detached, more purely entertaining fiction. It is what the title says, the story of a lost endeavour.

The story begins with the kidnapping and shipment into slavery of a Blackheath schoolboy, and of the French master from his school, in the year 1690. It tells of their separation and subsequent meeting in Virginia, their escapes, adventures among Indians and pirates in the South American regions which John Masefield writes of again and again. Does this sound like a juvenile adventure story? It is not. The kidnapped boy grows old for his years. The master develops into a mystic-fanatic, becomes a pirate, a man with a frantic mission, the quest for a treasure hoard. Quite early in the story, the boy, having escaped from slavery only to be enslaved elsewhere, gazes at the ship he is forced to board and has cause to reflect:

> I was to go back to the hateful life of the sea on board her. She was to be my prison; a college where I should learn vice; a temple where I should be consecrated to the gallows. I had long since ceased to expect to get back to my father in England. . . .

All through the story, the boy is haunted by the fear of becoming hardened to the criminal life. The former schoolmaster, the lunatic, carries him off on a venture which all but succeeds. It is a thrilling story and a powerful one. Nothing improbable happens; it reads naturally for all the exotic scenery and the adventurous tone. One of the few times when Masefield seems perturbed about, or seems to question, the existing order of life, is represented here. It is a story of youth, but of experience, not innocence.

Innocence is the note of *Jim Davis*, the boys' tale which comes as a sort of reverse side of the coin to *Lost Endeavour*. This is a story intended for boys as well as being about one, but (perhaps the test of a children's classic) it has no age-limit. The tone is not noticeably reduced for the occasion, the excitement is not noticeably worked up. What makes it a children's book is simply the note of innocence. It is a smuggling tale and, as in *Lost Endeavour*, seafaring and kidnapping come into it. But it is not the happy ending alone that makes *Jim Davis* an utterly different book from its predecessor. And it is not that there is no violence, danger, fear and failure in *Jim Davis*. It is just that the more evil reaches of the human soul are not here touched upon.

John Masefield seems to know exactly what is wanted for children's stories. His contributions to *Chatterbox* are vividly remembered amongst their generations. But it was not for another sixteen years that his most widely celebrated children's classic, *The Midnight Folk*, appeared. This wonderful fantasy about a small boy, hidden treasure, cats, witches, smugglers, is a children's book that is likely to endure. It can and should be, and for all I know is, read by adults as well as the young. It is very much a poet's book. The element of fantasy is given all the accessories of fact. Much fantastic literature, simply because it is fantasy, is hazy and ill-defined. *The Midnight Folk* is an example of how sharp and lucid fantasy can be when it is deliberately intagliated on the surface of realism.

It is a story in which one type of adventure piles on top of another, and the whole thing is enormously laid on. I doubt if Masefield ever made quite such a splash in any of his other writings. Some idea of how the phantasmagoric welter of events is made to mix with typical diurnal episodes and people of English village life, may be gained from the few paragraphs from the end of the book quoted below. The author winds up the narrative in the celebrated manner of telling, in one rapid flourish, what happens to everyone and everything:

Abner Brown paid all the fines. Mrs Pouncer left the district that afternoon.

Roper Bilges was discharged from his place for poaching. In

revenge, he and his brother, Sir Hassle's footman, poisoned all the otter hounds. For this they were sent to Dr Gubbins' Remedial Home for Scoundrels, where parts of them have been cut out, cleaned, and then put back; they are already much improved. . . .

The Squire will not buy any more otter hounds, otter hunting has therefore come to an end there. Water-rat and Otter have the river to themselves; they are very happy there, as the salmon have begun to come back.

Joe has taken the pledge, and is keeping it.

Bitem is very well. He has a fine summer lair in the hollow of Spring Hill. So far he has had one of my hens and three of my ducks this season. In the winter he goes down to the cave near the river where no hounds ever come. I hear him singing from time to time.

Blackmalkin and Greymalkin have turned over new leaves; but of course they will never be so nice as Nibbins, who is the nicest cat there is. . . .

Kay and Caroline Louisa are as happy as the day is long. Last year they went to spend the winter as the guests of the Dictator of Santa Barbara, where they had a most happy time. While they were there, the Archbishop showed them the treasure, or some of it, in use, as it had been of old, the candlesticks on the Altar, the images against the screens in the quire and the vessels in the side-chapels. . . . You may be sure that there is no more witchcraft in the house, nothing but peace and mirth all day and at night peace, the owls crying, the crickets chirping. . . .

The young hero of *The Midnight Folk* is Kay Harker, of the same pedigree as that Sard Harker about whom Masefield had written three years before, in the book that established his reputation as a novelist.

The post-1918 novels are distinguished from the earlier ones by their steadier, more measured, style. In fact, the prose style which the author used in *Sard Harker* is very much the same as that which he used in the 1950s. He became rather more felicitous, if anything, more urbane and easy; but the author of *St Katherine of Ledbury* (1951) is recognizable as the author of *Sard Harker* (1924). Now the element which has been constant in Masefield's prose throughout these years is one that can be found, in different forms but in essence the same, in other examples of English prose. It has a great deal to do with the temperament of the author, and sometimes comes roughly under the category of 'Addisonian'. I do not really think Masefield was quite so Addisonian as all that, but his view of life – that attitude to the world which I have already described, in Aldous Huxley's terms, as one in which 'objects seem *friendly*' – has certainly got its counterpart in the familiar, genial and dignified urbanity of Joseph Addison. Lionel Johnson once wrote of Addison along with Steele, Montaigne, Lamb and Browne, as being 'each in his way and measure . . . thus *friendly with the world*'.[1] More to our point, Lionel Johnson equates this type of mind with a specific type of prose writing. 'This temper,' he writes, 'is most commonly shown by your leisurely essayist, your writer of wayward genial disquisitions, your pleasant and generous moralist.' This list, Lionel Johnson added to the name of Stevenson. I think we could certainly add John Masefield.

It is perhaps in his essays that the resemblance to this accomplished, liberal and gentle strain in English letters is most apparent (see his essays on Blake, Crabbe and Chaucer, for example) and the resemblance is verified, as an exception proves a rule, by the elevation of the tone on occasion to a more impassioned plane (see his essay, *Poetry*).[2]

To return to Masefield's novels. *Sard Harker* begins to reveal the prose stylist in what might be called the 'felicitous' tradition, and this style, I feel, begins in *Sard Harker* to enhance the poet's genius for story-telling.

At the same time, the novel form demands rather more than the graceful balancing of sentences and paragraphs,

[1](Italics mine) Essay, *R.L. Stevenson* in *Post Liminium* (1912).
[2]*Poetry* (1931).

and there is a good deal of conversation in *Sard Harker*. As I showed in dealing with the narrative poems, and notably *The Everlasting Mercy*, Masefield uses dialogue with some skill. The practice of this in verse not only proves a salutary discipline when he comes to prose, its effect is near-poetic. Note how the following passage has a witty terseness, a to-and-fro rhythm, an economy quite beyond the normal range of prose expression:

'Has a Spanish lady come to this house to-day?'
'Yes, sir.'
'Is she at the house now?'
'Yes, sir,'
'What is her name, do you know?'
'Yes, sir.'
'What is her name?'
'What is her name?'
'Yes,' Sard said, 'what is her name?'
'What name?'
'The name she is called by: her surname.'
'Whose name?'
'The lady's name.'
'Which name? There's so many names.'
'The name of the Spanish lady who came to this house to-day.'
'Oh,' the man said, 'the name of the lady who came to this house to-day?'
'Yes, that is what I want to know; what is her name?'
'Yes, sir,' the negro said; 'now I know what you want. I didn't know for the first moment what you asked me about, but now I know. Oh, yes, sir. Look, sir, I'm making a basket:
            Put the withy there,
            Cross the withy, there,
            Jesus in the air . . .
Sir, forgive my asking, but have you a little bit of tobacco or a goddam cigarette?'

Dealing with the interaction of leading personalities in the story, Masefield is less successful. Solitude, endurance, suffering, he portrays excellently, and is especially convincing when describing physical pain. But the relationships between people, and particularly between men and women, he does not handle easily. In fact, he has never, so far as I know, either in prose or verse, handled well a situation involving a man and a woman in any relationship whatsoever. It is a great flaw but less of a flaw than it would be in a different kind of novelist. For Masefield is a novelist primarily concerned with external action rather than interaction. Many are the friendships he describes, it is true. But they are friendships predestined by the author. Nothing but death seems to happen to a friendship in Masefield's books, once it is sealed and settled by him. So we must not look for the study of relationships which are in any large manner personal. The love-story of *Sard Harker*, then, is by the way. The real story is the adventure (and I mean, too, the spiritual adventure) of one man on a dangerous quest through the wastes and exotic forests of South America. The novel is a kind of allegory, a kind of secular *Pilgrim's Progress*.

The descriptive passages, whether of people, of places or of wild creatures, are wonderfully eloquent and shrewd. *Odtaa* (1927) is a similar tale, but to me less interesting. Like most authors, Masefield is at his best when, having done one thing well, he next does something quite different. In 1929 *The Hawbucks* appeared. This book is closely associated with the *Reynard* country and the hunting districts of the West Midlands. It is a love story in one sense, but such a light-hearted one, so near-farcical in parts, that it is difficult to say whether the author was really serious. While less fantastic by far than Max Beerbohm's *Zuleika Dobson*, there is something of a less gloriously calculating and a more staid and tangible Zuleika about the squire's youngest daughter who is the joy and despair of every young man in the countryside bar none. The zest with which Miss Carrie Harridew is pursued, and by what a collection of oddments in the way of male youth, adds to the farcical aspect of the book. It is swift-moving and full of the open air in a 'Georgianesque' way. The merits of the work reside in various aspects of situation, but Masefield simply cannot depict women even in fun.

That is why *The Bird of Dawning* (1933) is so very attractive and successful. There are no women in it. Most of the qualities in which the poet excels appear in this lovely story of the China Tea Race in the last days of sailing ships. It recounts a mighty endeavour amid storms, wrecks and disaster; the race itself is superb, and above all other characters towers the incomparable ship *The Bird of Dawning* herself.

But there are, among the merchant seamen, some remarkable personalities ranging from the insult-flinging, perverse, withdrawn Captain Duntisbourne to a certain Bloody Bill China. There are some fine storm-scenes in this novel. Masefield always manages to convey the suddenness with which the weather overtakes a ship. He does not, as even Conrad does, over-prolong the impression he requires to create by indulging in picturesque language for several passages too long. One of the 'unities' of fiction seems to be a law that the description of an incident should not, if possible, take longer to read than the time supposed to be occupied by the incident itself. (But of course, like most laws of art, this one has been magnificently broken – see Proust, almost any page.) So that in *The Bird of Dawning*, by so few words as those which follow, we are told of a suspected storm and its onslaught:

> Something ugly was coming on from south and west. Its advance guards, of a swell upon the sea, a closeness upon the air, and a madness upon the human nerve, were already upon them. Gradually, the air, so hot and damp, became denser, till it was liker steam than air. The noises of the water in the freeing-ports, the gear jangling, the kick of the wheel, and the swirl about the rudder, even the low voices of men in the waist talking

about times ashore, became more and more audible, till they were nearly unendurable. The horizon dimmed itself out; the sky that had been starry, and then pallid, became obscured. Cruiser felt suddenly that it was 'coming on thick'.

It came very quickly and very gently, in little drifts of greyness like wool, each not much bigger, as it seemed, than the mottling in cirro-cumulus. They came in about the ship seemingly from the south and west, but upon an unfelt breath. At one minute they were not there, and he could see the sea dark, oily, and gleaming from the side lights: in the next minute they were the world.

Another beautifully-told tale is *The Taking of the Gry* (1934) (again a more or less all-male cast), describing a 1911 revolution in the Spanish Main. It is told in the first person, a method in which Masefield achieved his happiest results where the novel is concerned.

In 1936 and 1937 were published two novels called respectively *Eggs and Baker* and *The Square Peg*, both of them dealing with English country life in times of social change.

The first of these novels is placed in the 1870s and is filled with highly interesting detail which the author's prodigious and scholarly industry has not only acquired, in all accuracy, but on which he has brought to bear a powerful historical imagination. This book contains some good incidents – particularly a court trial. Masefield is very good on trials. *Eggs and Baker* (sub-titled *The Days of Trial*) is a story of people concerned, in different ways, with social reform. These include a country baker and his family (a baker not dissimilar from the miller in Hardy's *Trumpet Major*), and a 'professional' social reformer of a very bleak type (a reformer suggestively named Engels, though the other Engels had more tact than his fictitious namesake). Though Masefield's historical insight is profoundly keen throughout, the work suffers from that inconclusiveness which frequently marks the liberal mind; the conclusion of the tale simply leaves aloft all the issues previously raised.

The Square Peg is a twentieth-century tale featuring the descendant, Robert Mansell, of the baker Robert Mansell of *Eggs and Baker*. It is located in the same district. There is a unity between these books and others which incorporate members of the same family – a unity which is not so obvious as that, for instance, of the 'Forsyte' books. By using the same family names for his characters and the same county scenes, names of villages and towns, Masefield manages to convey the continuity of his background, the continuity of certain tendencies of character, along with the individualism of certain people in their complete difference from their ancestors. The books are therefore not, strictly, sequels.

The Square Peg or The Gun Fella is a satirical commentary on the encroachments of the middle class on the preserves of the landed class, the invasion of the land by industry. Apart from the incidents dealing with his hero's love affairs, Masefield gives us here a most amusing and penetrating critique of the times. The country gentry are shown as a mixed company. Some of the people from *Reynard the Fox* turn up again and they are all set down with what seems entire justice, from the generous and courteous Sir Peter Bynd to the local Bright Young People. The virtues and vices of this fox-hunting set are equally exposed with the merits and demerits of Robert Mansell, the inventor of an ingenious, fatal and cheap machine-gun called Mansell's Deadly Death Rose. This clever young man is a denouncer of fox-hunting as a cruel sport. Mansell's acquisition of a country house, his prevention of fox-hunting on his land and the mean measures taken by the local gentry to remove him are a joy to read, for the tone is one of restrained levity all along. But here again we are up against Masefield's inability, or refusal, to take sides. The liberal temperament which so delightfully carries off a tale like *Reynard the Fox*, where no social issue is at stake, is simply evasive in a story like *The Square Peg*. I do not mean that it is not an excellent story, for as always with Masefield the best of the tale is in the telling of it. The prose is

in the author's most pleasant style. It is by far his most
humorous work. He brings insight and judgment to his
characters as individuals, but judgment, final judgment on
their actions he just will not pass. Some people prefer it that
way, in the tradition which John Galsworthy represents.

My own preference is for Masefield's later adventure
stories, where the issues involved are not between social
classes but between individuals, or between men and
circumstances, or men and nature. By this time he had
perfected his style of prose so that it admirably suited the
needs of such stories. And in 1938 he wrote what I consider
his best prose work, *Dead Ned*. This was followed the next
year by a sequel (*Live and Kicking Ned*).

Dead Ned – attractively sub-titled *The Autobiography of a
Corpse* – was inspired by a tale told to Masefield when he was
dining at the now blitzed Barbers' Hall, and personally
recounted to me:

It appears that it was once the custom for bodies of hanging
criminals to be brought from Tyburn to be dissected by the
surgeon-barbers. Now among this noble Company there
existed a pact that if any hanged body, not quite a corpse,
should be brought in, all efforts should be made to restore life.
As the Law would, in such a case, demand the return of the
wretched criminal to be re-hanged, it was agreed upon by this
compassionate band of surgeons that the escape should be
facilitated of any hanged men brought back to life.

The Worshipful Company of Barbers maintain a legend to
this day that a screen in their possession, which Masefield
said was shown to him, was sent to them by a grateful
'resurrected man', one of those who had been smuggled out
of the country. Whether it was to the Bight of Benin in the
Gulf of Guinea that this unfortunate young man was sent,
like Masefield's Dead Ned, I do not know.

Masefield fully exploits the dramatic potentialities of this
story. The subject of hanging, which the poet has treated in
other works, is here wholly mastered from the artistic point

of view. The poet's imaginative identification with Ned Mansell (an earlier member of the Mansell family), in his dying and in his resuscitation, is achieved with emphatic conviction. The scene of Ned's trial, the scenes at Newgate jail, the description of Ned's disguise and flight under pursuit, are what one remembers most vividly. There are some memorable portraits here too, so real that one feels they must be composite pictures of people Masefield has met at different times in his life. For example, all of the Admiral's characteristics and cranks escape the 'fictionalized' air that so many story-book eccentrics possess; and then there is the servant Henry, so sly, so pitiable, so vicious a being; there is Ned's father, weak and strong in curious ways. Above all, *Dead Ned* carries a tragic sense of mystery which seems to transcend even the horror. Though Ned is revived by the surgeons after being hanged, though he escapes and survives the horrors of the slave trade, though, in the sequel, he is even acquitted of the crime for which he was hanged, this one terrible event, the hanging, enfolds his life and sets him forever apart from his fellow-men. The tragic note on which the book is pitched is implicit in Ned's words:

> There are relatives of my mother still alive. I saw and talked with two of them a fortnight ago. If they had thought that I was I, they would have swooned. But I am Dead Ned; I do not exist; I am never talked of; I am forgotten.

I consider *Dead Ned* the peak of the poet's achievement in fiction. His later prose work, notably the semi-historical *Badon Parchments* (a tale of early Britain) and *Conquer* (a tale of the Nika rebellion in Byzantium) attempt to do different things. They are essentially tales of events, whereas *Dead Ned* is the story of a man. *Basilissa*, a novel based on a theme similar to that of *Conquer*, is the story of a young woman dancer of Byzantium and her historic progress; I do not think it succeeds.

So I end with *Dead Ned*, the lovely story in which recurs so strikingly the couplet:

> Beware, beware, the Bight of Benin,
> Few come out, though many go in.

In response to a question about *Dead Ned*, Masefield repeated these lines so eagerly that I wonder if the book was not inspired as much by the couplet as by the strange story from Barbers' Hall.

John Masefield's achievements in fiction are, essentially, a poet's. He uses words with the utmost sensitivity. He occupies himself and engages the reader in the minutiae of every phenomenon he undertakes to write about – the smallest details of any profession or craft of mankind belonging to any period in history or any place are not overlooked by him. In this way he gets at the essentials of a situation, perhaps paradoxically. That is Masefield's secret. Some novelists lay bare their story by making the broad, generalizing sweep. Some concentrate on dialogue to bring forth the essence of their tale. Masefield goes into detail after detail until the reader is closely acquainted with the subject of the story, and until the relevance of those details, carefully, deliberately chosen after all, becomes apparent, and the essence of Masefield's world, simple and noble, emerges.

Selected Books by John Masefield

POEMS

Salt Walter Ballads, 1902

Ballads and Poems, 1903: *revised* 1910

The Everlasting Mercy, 1911

Dauber, 1913

Sonnets and Poems, 1916

Lollingdon Downs and other Poems, 1917

Reynard the Fox, 1919

Right Royal, 1920

Minnie Maylow's Story, 1931

Collected Poems; *enlarged edn.*, 1938 (*including the above works, in part or entire*)

On the Hill, 1949

PLAYS

The Tragedy of Nan, 1909

The Tragedy of Pompey the Great, 1910

Good Friday, 1916

The Locked Chest/The Sweeps of Ninety-Eight, 1916

Esther, *adapted from Racine*, 1922

Berenice, *adapted from Racine*, 1922

FICTION

A Tarpaulin Muster, 1907

Captain Margaret, 1908

Lost Endeavour, 1910

FICTION – *cont.*

Jim Davis, 1911

Sard Harker, 1924

Odtaa, 1927

The Midnight Folk, 1927

The Hawbucks, 1929

The Bird of Dawning, 1933

Eggs and Baker, 1936

The Square Peg, 1937

Dead Ned, 1938

Live and Kicking Ned, 1939

GENERAL

On the Spanish Main, 1906

Shakespeare, 1911

Gallipoli, 1916

St. George and the Dragon, 1919 (*lectures*)

The Battle of the Somme, 1919

Recent Prose, 1924 (*selected essays*)

The Wanderer of Liverpool, 1930

Poetry: a Lecture, 1931

The Nine Days' Wonder, 1941

A Book of Both Sorts, 1947 (*selected poetry and prose*)

St Katherine of Ledbury, 1951

AUTOBIOGRAPHY

In the Mill, 1941

New Chum, 1944

So Long to Learn, 1952